Turning Around a Bank in Korea

A business and cultural challenge

By

Robert A. Cohen

Turning Around a Bank in Korea
A business and cultural challenge

Published by Lulu.com

ISBN 978-0-557-03772-8

First edition: December 2008

Printed in the United States of America

Contents

Acknowledgments

I owe many thanks to many people for the great job done in Korea.

Firstly, I would like to thank my beloved wife, Annie. We have been married for thirty-six years. I made her travel a lot on three continents, and I believe she was quite settled in New York when this Korean opportunity arose. She accepted immediately, leaving, for the first time, our two children. I know these three-and-a-half years were not easy for her. She felt she was very far from our family and our friends, distance wise and also by the time difference. It is difficult to keep phone relations with thirteen hours difference. It was from then on she became an email adept.
I know she enjoyed tremendously the cultural discovery of Korea and the lively art scene, but I also know how frustrated she was by the lack of communication, the language, and the socio-cultural difference. Without her approval nothing would have been possible.

Secondly, I want to thank David Bonderman and his team of TPG Newbridge, especially Dan Carroll and Weijian Shan, for their confidence. They gave me the opportunity and all along showed me their support after direct and lively discussions.

Thirdly, I want to thank the expatriate executives who were lured to Korea First Bank (KFB) by my predecessor and

TPG Newbridge prior to my arrival who stayed and worked with me: Duncan Barker, chief operating officer; Ranvir Dewan, chief financial officer; S. H. Lee, chief credit officer; Jay Hyun, chief information officer; and Keith Shachat, chief of retail risks. A bank turnaround cannot be done without a cohesive team.

I want to give a special mention to my friend, Duncan Barker, who was instrumental in the transformation of KFB and has been with a great patience my English support. I decided to write this book in English and not in French, my mother tongue, because I thought that most of the interested readers would speak English. These readers' experiences would be much more painful without Duncan's patient correcting job. I am afraid I have damaged his perfect Scottish English. All remaining errors are definitely of my fault and only my fault.

Fourthly, I would like to include in my thanks KFB's Korean officers and employees. A bank is a service company and cannot work well without cohesion. Like in a rowboat, everybody has to row in the same direction to have it go straight ahead, and that was only possible because they trusted me and accepted and followed the strange instructions of a just arrived French chief executive officer (CEO) who was speaking English with a thick accent.

Many Korean officers played a major role in the turnaround. It is impossible for me to name them all, but to name only few: Mr. J. H. Kim, the human resources manager; Mr. H. T. Park, who managed the whole sale mortgage division; Mr. D. H. Cho, who took care of the management reporting; Mr. H. P. Kim, the chairman of the union, so many discussions, oppositions, and negotiations have built our mutual respect and friendship.

I would especially like to thank S. Y. Yang, who managed the retail network. He was instrumental in its transformation and now is my friend.

I would like also to thank J. Y. Chang, an extraordinary lawyer who is a partner with Kim and Chang, who has spent hundreds of hours with me helping me understand and live with the Korean legal and regulatory system.

Last, but not least, I would like to thank my closest supports, my secretary, N. S. Cha, and my always smiling and helpful driver, Mr. Kim. Above all, my main interpreters: Christine, who translated for me the first year, and Cecile, who subsequently took her position and was de facto my closest support, so close that my wife nicknamed her "my first wife," hinting that Cecile was spending more time with me than she did. Cecile was both my ear and my voice! The precision of her immediate oral translation was capital, letting me understand and react to the slightest nuances. Any mistake in translating my words would have been highly confusing for my interlocutors on the other side, especially in the tense and long negotiations with the unions and the long but capital speeches I made in front of the bank's officers. Cecile was always behind me. From breakfast to dinner she was the perfect and indispensable support.

Introduction

By Dr. Weijian Shan

"David, I have just signed all the definitive agreements!" I could hardly conceal my relief and excitement as I spoke by phone with David Bonderman, co-chairman of Newbridge Capital and a founding partner of TPG.

"Congratulations," came David's voice. "Now the hard part has begun!"

This conversation took place on December 23, 1999. The easy part, by Bonderman's implication, took fifteen months of grueling negotiations that at times seemed to be heading nowhere or completely dead. The final agreement was finally reached (please pardon the pun) for Newbridge Capital, the investment firm I represented, to acquire control of Korea First Bank, a failed and subsequently nationalized bank, from the Korean government.

The date of the final signing was not accidental. I had earlier declared to the representatives of the Korean government that I would not spend another Christmas in Seoul. Both sides had been completely exhausted by then and knew that we probably never would if we couldn't get it done before the second Christmas since the beginning of the negotiations. We were, to be sure, getting very close, and a level of trust had developed between the two sides after so many months being the bane of each other's existence. A deadline strongly motivated the two teams to work even harder. Just then, the legal team representing the government declared that there was no way the deadline could be met because they had worked for forty-eight hours straight without any sleep, and to continue was humanly impossible.

I was gripped by despair. We were getting so close! After an hour of pacing the floors of Shilla Hotel, where both teams were camped out in its business center for many days and nights, I came up with a totally crazy idea: I proposed to the leader of the Korean team to second one of our lawyers to his team to help complete documentation of the final agreements. To my surprise, even though I had a slim hope he would, he accepted it.

Thus Newbridge Capital took over control of Korea First Bank. We would invest $500 million to own 51 percent of KFB. The Korean government, through the Ministry of Finance and Economy, Financial Supervisory Commission, and KDIC, would own the remaining 49 percent, but we would have 100 percent voting rights.

Korea First Bank was one of the major national banks in South Korea that had failed during the Asian financial crisis of 1997–98. Before then, South Korea had almost forty years of uninterrupted, rapid industrialization and economic growth led by large conglomerates, known in Korean as *chaebol*. The chaebols, such as Daewoo, Hyundai, and Samsung, had rapidly expanded not only domestically but also globally. By the mid-1990s, the chaebols had become household names in western markets.

The growth of chaebol was helped, very crucially, by Korean banks that, guided by the policies of the government, continuously provided credit and funding to the chaebols to the extent not seen anywhere else in the world. By 1998, the average debt-equity ratio for large Korean firms became an astounding five times, whereas the comparable ratio for American firms was well below one. That meant that for every dollar of capital, a chaebol was able to borrow five dollars of debt from banks. This also meant if for some reason the cash flow generated by the chaebol could not meet the debt obligation to the banks, there was no way the debt could be paid back as the capital, or net asset value, was only a fraction of the debt obligation. It seemed that nobody had worried about this possibility with unthinkable implications for Korean banks as the failure of a large chaebol, always supported by government policies, was unthinkable. They were just too big to fail.

The unthinkable happened in 1997, beginning with what appeared to be a relative small event: the devaluation of the Thai baht on July 2, 1997. This triggered a financial crisis as international investors, fearing a domino effect, pulled money out of other Asian markets. As investors rushed to the door, the currencies of several Asian countries, from South Korea to Indonesia, collapsed in value, which in turn accelerated the capital flight. By the end of 1997, the capital markets in Asia were completely seized up, and capital became very scarce. Previously, many Korean firms had to borrow to pay back their earlier borrowings. Now the credit market dried up, and Korean banks could no longer lend. As one after another Korean firms failed, their banks could no longer recover the money lent to these firms. Yet, they needed the money to pay back the depositors from whom banks collected money in the first place. Banks began to fail.

Korea First Bank was one of the first victims of this rapidly developing vicious cycle but fundamentally also a victim of a lending policy that followed government policies without focusing on the credit-worthiness of the borrower. Korean banking was typical policy lending or relationship lending. There was a great lack of a credit culture, that focused on the borrower's credit or ability to pay back a loan, as is customary in international best practices of banking.

As a condition for a financial rescue package for South Korea of about $58 billion, the Korean government agreed with the International Monetary Fund to sell Korea First Bank and Seoul Bank, another failed and subsequently nationalized bank, to foreign investors. The reason to do so, from the point of view of the IMF, was to bring in international best practices in banking and a credit culture. This condition was painful for Korea, which until then had never allowed foreign control of a Korean bank. Eventually, after almost two years of on and off negotiations, the plan to also sell Seoul Bank to a foreign bank was scraped.

On a morning in October 1998 I was getting into a car with Dan Carroll, my partner at Newbridge Capital, when the hotel receptionist handed me a stack of faxes. Dan and I were in New York City fund-raising. One of the faxes, as I read aloud, came from Paul Chen from Hong Kong. He advised us that the Korean government had begun a formal process of auctioning off two failed and then nationalized banks, Korea First Bank and Seoul Bank. We were in the depth of a financial crisis in Asia, and South Korea was one of the hardest hit countries. Who in his right mind would want to buy a failed bank in the middle of a financial meltdown?

"Before we turn it down," Dan suggested, "why don't we send it to David Bonderman to see what he thinks?"

David and his partners acquired American Savings Bank from the U.S. federal government in the savings and loan crisis of the late 1980s, pioneered a model to separate the good assets of the bank from the bad (the good bank, bad bank model), turned it around, and eventually made a killing in financial rewards.

David never fails to return a message within twenty-four hours, sooner if you live in the same time zone with him. He began, in characteristically Bonderman style, "The history of life shows that if you structure a deal right, this is about the best time to buy a bank."

Thus began our long journey to acquire and eventually turn around Korea First Bank. I flew to Seoul as soon as I returned to Asia from America.

At mid-2001 we came to another critical juncture in the turning around of KFB. In the first year of our control KFB made money, whereas the previous year the bank lost billions of dollars, mostly due to the write-off of bad loans representing as much as 50 percent of all the outstanding loans. Before it failed, KFB was largely a corporate bank whose customers were mostly large corporations such as Daewoo, Hanbo Steel, Kia Motors, and the like. It was the failure of these large corporations that also doomed KFB. Now under our control and the leadership of the new board, KFB sharply pulled back from lending to large corporate customers, many of which were too heavily leveraged or indebted and were so severely affected by the financial crisis they were in poor financial condition. Fearful of risk concentration to some large corporate customers like KFB used to have, the new board imposed a house rule that the management had to seek and obtain the approval of the board if lending to any single customer was to exceed $100 million. Furthermore, the new management steered the bank sharply away from corporate lending and in the direction of retail banking by providing retail customers with such products as mortgage loans.

KFB, under the new management, also became the only Korean bank able to resist the pressure by the government to help bail out troubled companies and to lend to weak credits or to those whose ability to pay back a loan was dubious. While KFB was fortunate to maintain its independence in credit decision making from potential government interference or influence, there was no denying that the new management of KFB had to endure much social pressure for being the only one in Korea to repeatedly say no to the government and to refuse to play ball like the rest of the banking industry.

Then in late spring 2001 we discovered the management extended a loan of about $200 million to the troubled Hynix, a semiconductor manufacturer, as part of the rescue package orchestrated by the relevant authorities. The management finally succumbed to pressure from the authorities and became part of the rescue. I suppose being the lone resistance to such pressures for so long must have made them feel like social outcasts, which motivated them to make it back into the circle by doing in Rome as the Romans did. In any case, there was little doubt that the management was also quite convinced by the financial advisor of Hynix that the risks of this lending were manageable. In violation of the house rule, the management didn't seek board approval for doubling the limit of lending to a single borrower. The board only became aware of this large risk when Hynix, unable to service its debt, came back for another round of borrowing from all of its banks, including KFB. Our board refused. The decision was undoubtedly correct, because in spite of the coordinated efforts by its creditors, the previous loans made to Hynix eventually had to be written off. It was a big loss to KFB, which otherwise had maintained a great credit risk control policy since our takeover.

We needed a new CEO. We needed someone of integrity and good reputation who had managed a large banking operation, who the board could immediately trust, who was willing to live in Korea, and who would command respect by our Korean government partner and by KFB's employees. A new CEO, however tested and experienced in his previous job, always brings a huge amount of uncertainty to the organization, because no matter how much experience he has had, it remains uncertain if he will be successful in a new organization in a new environment. The task of finding the right person was urgent and yet very daunting.

All the visiting board members were staying at Seoul's Shilla Hotel. I was having breakfast in the hotel café with my partner, Paul Chen, who had worked closely with me on the KFB transaction, and we were discussing where to find such a perfect candidate.

Suddenly Paul blurted out, "How about Robert Cohen?"

It is like someone switched on a light in my head, and my eyes immediately lit up:

"That is a very good idea. Why, a perfect idea!"

We all knew Robert Cohen very well by now. Robert was invited to join the board of KFB by David Bonderman, who had known Robert for a long time. Robert came with impeccable credentials as a veteran banking leader. He was vice chairman of Republic National Bank of New York before he retired. Before then, he was the chief executive officer of Credit Lyonnais USA, also with responsibilities for the whole of the Americas. Robert was also an intellectual. An alumnus of the French elite school Ecole Polytechnique with a PhD in finance from University Paris Dauphine, he taught economics and finance in French graduate schools for sixteen years. With this rare combination of academic background and practitioner's experiences, Robert not only knew banking inside and out, but also knew how to manage a large banking operation in different cultures.

We all appreciated and respected Robert as one of the most diligent members of the board of KFB. He had made constant contributions to the board discussions since day one. He invariably read every page of piles of board meeting materials before every board meeting. He knew every subject and every number by heart. His comments and suggestions were always very thoughtful and thought provoking. He offered new ideas and new perspectives not thought of by others. For example, from very early on, he recommended to the board and the management that we make the maturity of KFB's assets longer than it was as he expected interest rates to fall in Korea. Later events proved him to be completely correct. The bank would have been more profitable if the management followed his advice on the asset mix.

We also knew that Robert and his wife had taken a strong interest in Korean culture since they first visited.

But Korea isn't a popular destination for western businessmen, and the expatriate community in Seoul is very small. It is almost impossible to communicate in English (and certainly not in French, Robert's mother tongue) on the streets of Seoul. The working language of KFB was predominantly Korean, which Robert didn't speak. We had no idea if Robert would be interested in such a difficult job and in moving his family to Seoul.

I called Robert in his room and invited him out for a walk in the hills behind Shilla Hotel.

"We have a problem," I began.

I was about to get into my prepared speech about the challenges we faced to find, in a hurry, a new CEO whose credentials had to be above any shred of a doubt by multiple constituencies including the board, the Korean government, employees, customers, and the public media. But before I could continue, Robert interrupted me:

"Do you think I am the solution to your problem?"

"Why, yes. Of course, that is if you are interested in considering it," I said.

"I am interested, but I need to talk with my wife, Annie," Robert said.

I also needed to speak with my other partners and with Bob Barnum, chairman of the board, although I was quite confident that all would be delighted if Robert was willing to take the job. They were. When I called David Bonderman and Richard Blum, my other co-chairman of

Newbridge Capital, they both thought it would be great if Robert was willing to serve. They were both surprised—pleasantly, however—that Robert had already said yes.

How would a French CEO fare in a Korean organization?

"Well," Richard Blum said, "at least they have something in common. They don't speak each other's languages, but they all speak English as a foreign language."

Our confidence in Robert Cohen aside, what he took on was indeed a huge challenge, as he would soon discover.

Reflections of a Trailing Spouse

By Annie S. Cohen

"Bad timing! Very bad timing!"

This was pretty much all I could think of that evening when my husband sat with me to discuss the job offer he was seriously considering accepting.

I had traveled with him to Korea this time. The summertime was finished in New –York; Labor Day week-end was over, and our children were in the city, either back to work or just out of college and looking for a job. Why not accept my husband's suggestion to join him on his business trip? I love Asia and was thrilled to get a chance to spend some time away from Manhattan visiting museums and shopping as he was attending the board meeting of Korea First Bank.

It was the month of September, and the fall was glorious in Seoul after the very long rainy season, a beautiful, crispy, end of summer that I was in no mood to appreciate. We had left New York four days before, and I was still trying to absorb the thirteen-hour time difference, but that had nothing to do with the fact I felt totally numb.

It was September 13, 2001.

I was stunned. I was scared. I could hardly process any more information. I just couldn't wait to be back home where I belonged, hug my children, and grieve with my fellow New Yorkers.

What was he saying?

He had been offered to work as CEO of Korea First Bank. It implied living in Seoul; it would be for a certain number of years. Would I agree to move?

It felt so weird, so surreal. I knew it was important to him, a challenge he felt ready to take on.
I keep thinking that I was so much in shock from the terrorist attack that had just happened two days earlier that I didn't quite grasp all the consequences of agreeing to move to Korea.

I left New York by the end of December 2001. It was painful because of the circumstances and the uncertainty about the future that prevailed at that time in New York City.

My Korean life was beginning, and I am very thankful for this unexpected experience.

Suddenly transformed into a *samonim*, a Korean lady with all the social privileges attached to this title, I was a member of a very rarefied group: the non-Korean wives of non-Korean CEOs of Korean companies.

Not only was I not in Kansas anymore, I was not in Central Park either.

When your answering machine talks back to you in Japanese, your microwave is totally underused because you can't understand the directions, the lovely flowers delivered to your home are not for you but for your husband and come with a large ribbon all written in Chinese, the TV has an HBO channel that shows movies in Russian, Japanese, or Chinese subtitled in Korean, you know you are asking for trouble.

It was actually quite refreshing to have to shake up my comfortable American habits and to open my eyes to a new reality in my new persona—exasperating sometimes, frustrating often, funny more often, but above all exciting.

Leaving home was an adventure already. I was analphabet; I couldn't read or speak Korean.

With some time and perseverance I learned to read Korean and spoke enough to be polite which allowed me to function in my daily life, approximately.

This was a fascinating learning experience to me. I fell in love with the beauty of the mountains, the isolated Buddhist temples, the stunning spirituality of the rock carvings in the 1000 Buddha Mountain, the magic of the lantern processions, the amazing perfection of the antique Korean ceramics, the elegance of the *Hanbock*, the beautiful national costume.

It was a privilege to spend those few years in Korea and to be able to open a window into this culture.

It was even more so because it was a discovery I was sharing with my husband.

"Wherever you go, I'll go."

I took it seriously.

Introduction to Korea

Korea, a Little Known Country

My wife, our two children, and I have lived in France, Belgium, and New York, and I have traveled extensively both for business and leisure. I have been in most of the American and West European countries and many Asian and African countries also.
I have visited many times Japan, China, Hong Kong, Thailand, Indonesia, and Australia, but never Korea, and I should admit my knowledge about Korea was close to zero.

I discovered quickly that I was not the exception but the general rule. No one really gets to know Korea without having spent a few years there. In fact, the only ones talking about Korea in the USA were the veterans, and of course their memories were understandably dramatic and with very little relevance to modern-day Korea. This image was so strong that I was unable in 2000 to find any recent travel guide about Korea in New York, and I found only one in France of all places! The French people knew even less about Korea than the Americans, but not having been traumatized by the Korean War, there was one travel book. The least we can say is that it was a very exclusive edition.

So why is Korea this mystery?

I gradually began to understand it as I will try to explain in the following chapters. It is a mix of many elements: the geographical situation far from the main roads; the peculiarity of Korean history which isolated the country for so long; the direct actions of its neighbors; and its cultural insularity and poverty, at least until the 1990s.

This last element is very important, and we will come back to it. Every visitor or foreigner who lived in Korea in the 1960s and 1970s would paint a picture of a country totally different from Korea today. Changes there have come faster and been more dramatic than anywhere else in the world.

So, it was without any personal knowledge (which meant also without any bias) that my wife and I went to Korea, open minded but without expectations; thinking that relations would be difficult, especially with the double barrier of language and culture. We were both under the reality—and dead wrong!

To help you understand better this story, as well as the Korea First Bank one together with our interaction with Koreans, I thought it might be useful in this introduction to put a few things in the Korean context, namely the history, the demographics, religion, and the economy, even though it took us months to get at this level of understanding.

Korea's History

Korea has a long and very specific history. Nobody can possibly understand Koreans without having studied their history and its effects on this very homogeneous population. My purpose here is not to give a detailed history lesson, but to help better understand Koreans and their culture.

Korea is a peninsula situated between China and Japan. It is a cold country in the winter, very mountainous, and with few plains.

Until the seventh century, Korea was separated into three kingdoms: the north, the southeast, and the southwest. In the eighth century, the southeast kingdom (or Shilla) unified the country with Kyangju as its capital. From there, other dynasties followed the Unified Shilla, including Goryo (tenth to fourteenth centuries), and then Chosun (from the end of the fourteenth century until the nineteenth century). It was during this time that the capital was moved to Seoul.

Relations with its neighbors had a major effect on Korea history.

China, the great neighbor, tried many times to move the border to its advantage, but the Koreans succeeded in maintaining their land, and so this lopsided relation endured.

China was careful to keep Korea in a vassal position, forbidding it to import any crucial new products or practices. For example, it is commonly reported that China did not allow Korea to import cotton plants for centuries until a Korean succeeded in smuggling three cotton plants inside the hollow handle of a brush! Naturally, Chinese policy slowed Korean development, as you will see.

Japan had even more impact on Korea, and not for the better.

During the Shilla and Goryo Dynasties, Korea was clearly more civilized than Japan, itself an island with even fewer trading relations than Korea. In fact, the Japanese acted similar to the Vikings in France, attacking by boat, killing, burning, and taking whatever they wanted, whether it was women, valuables, or even skills. During the Goryo Dynasty, the Koreans achieved a spectacular level in making Celadon pottery. The Japanese hijacked most of those artists back to Japan to develop their own pottery industry. Interestingly, there is still a Korean colony in Japan, said to be the descendants of these hijacked potters, not even integrated after seven centuries!

In the sixteenth century, the Japanese invaded Korea and destroyed many cities, including many palaces and temples... At the end of the nineteenth century, Japan invaded Korea again and this time stayed until the end of World War II. During this long occupation, their policy was to fully annex Korea, replacing Korean culture and identity with Japan's, and of course, many remnants of Korea's past history were tragically destroyed.

Following into more modern times, the Korean War and the resultant bifurcation of the country were extremely traumatic for the nation, causing destruction, enormous casualties, dislocation of families, and then a difficult new start for the Republic of Korea, as we know it today.

Korea was always a tough place to live. There are few plains, with long and very cold winters. There were few cattle, no sheep and so no wool, and no cotton. Koreans wore linen, silk (at least for the wealthiest), and hemp. This was obviously not enough to fight the cold, and many were dying prematurely of cold, even into the second half of the twentieth century. Food was also scarce, especially in winter. Being on a peninsula without cattle and few plains to grow cereals, the Koreans survived on vegetables, fish, sea food, barley, and rice for the wealthiest.

To survive the winter, they developed the art of drying fish and squid. In today's Korea, westerners are always surprised to see mostly dried fish, which is more salty. The Koreans understandably value these dried fishes much more than fresh ones. In America or Europe, modern life with refrigerators and widely available fresh products began at least three generations ago. In Korea, this was introduced only one generation ago, not long enough to have changed tastes or habits.

The same applies for preserving vegetables. The traditional way was making kimchi. Every year before winter set in, the women in every family prepared (and still prepare) huge pots of kimchi. Usually made with cabbage (but sometimes radishes or onions), salt, red peppers, spices, and small shrimps, this mixture would be kept outside in breathing earthenware partly buried in the ground, and as a result of natural fermentation would be kept safe to eat for years if needed. This tradition, so vital in keeping the vegetables through the long winters, is widely maintained today and has developed into one of the most iconic staples of Korean cuisine. Very few Koreans can imagine breakfast, lunch, or dinner without kimchi. Here also, the refrigerators and freezers widely used today in Korea have failed to change this tradition and method of preparation.

Korea was at its height during the Shilla and Goryo Dynasties. Certainly at that time it was among the advanced nations with the very early invention and use of printing, first with woodblocks and then with separate letters (early thirteenth century), the mastering of the arts of pottery, paper, and painting. But the limited exposure to foreigners, due partly to its neighbors' policies and the need to protect itself in front of these two powers limited its progress. On the eve of the Japanese invasion at the end of the nineteenth century, the country was poor—barely at subsistence level—with a life expectancy lower than thirty years old, mostly due to the bitter cold as well as malnutrition.

After more than fifty years of a tough occupation and the Korean War which happened shortly thereafter, Korea had little to show and was not much more prosperous. The country was divided by the armistice, and so from this point forward I will use the term Korea to mean The Republic of Korea or South Korea. North Korea is an enigma to me, and so I do not feel qualified to discuss it, and Korea First Bank had no activity there.

In the 1960s Korea was still extremely poor, poorer than many African countries at that time, with a gross domestic product (GDP) per capita of only US$100 in 1963. The rigorous climate was still the cause of many deaths, in spite of the intensive use of wood burning (which nearly destroyed all the forests). Life expectancy was about forty!

People born in the 1950s still acutely remember searching for enough food to feed their families and fighting the cold to survive, definitely not the memories that most of their counterparts in Europe or America have today.

A few strong leaders pushed the country toward industrial development in a militaristic fashion, and it was only in the last twenty years that democracy actually developed. Democracy is today already very well rooted and recent events, including the tentative process of impeachment of the president in 2003, have shown that Korea's democracy is remarkably strong at such a young age.

Korea's Peculiar Demography

When we arrived in Korea, my wife and I were stunned to see how young the crowds seemed in the streets, in the movie theatres, and in the restaurants.

We felt old among all these young people!

At the end of the Korean War the life expectancy was around forty. Only a small minority survived above the age of sixty among the ones born before the 1960s. And today, there are only a small number of people older than seventy. Thanks to the rapid growth in the economy and medicine, life expectancy has increased progressively from forty to more than seventy in only forty years! For Europe and the

United States, it took two hundred years to arrive at this level.

The result is a population with fewer elderly people but one that is aging quickly. The forty- and fifty-year-olds today should now survive to reach eighty. That is totally new in a country where a sixtieth birthday was so rare that it was celebrated like a new birth, more or less what can be compared in New York to a one hundredth birthday celebration.

In many large corporations the retirement age is around sixty, but strong social pressure pushes people above fifty to think of themselves as elderly and thus take early retirement. This approach was perfectly reasonable in the 1970s and 1980s, when the life expectancy was around sixty at best, but is it still acceptable today? On this subject, collective and individual behavior shows that they cannot change as fast as the economy.

On the other hand, the Koreans have learned quickly in terms of family size. In the old days as in Europe a few centuries ago, many children were produced to ensure some survived to adulthood. Today, medicine and development have practically eradicated infant mortality. But the fear of poverty, the cost of education, and the willingness to grow on the social scale very quickly pushed the Koreans to reduce the number of children to a worrisome level, well under what is needed to keep on the long term the same level of population.

As a result, we are seeing a population, today young, aging faster than most by cumulating a drastic reduction of the number of children with a structural increase of the number of the oldest. .An evolution of two centuries in western developed countries has occurred in one generation in Korea. We will continue to see the multiple consequences of this extraordinary acceleration in the years to come.

- Confucianism and Tradition

Korea was a deeply Buddhist country but also was the country the most influenced by Confucius, even more than China. The result is very strong traditions made stronger by the isolation of Korea until recently and the defiance towards foreign traditions, which is understandable when we know the history of its relations with its neighbors.

The first aspect is respect for seniority, virtually cult like when applied to ancestors.

The authority of elders in the family cannot be challenged; the young people have to follow. Until recently, couples would have the parents of the husband living with them and would show to the elder man the most respect and obedience. Unthinkable in western culture, the young wife will not even dare to go to bed (or even go to the bathroom) until her father-in-law is himself sleeping. Changes are occurring slowly with longer life expectancy and urbanization, but the hierarchy is still very apparent.

Regardless of family ties, the Koreans show respect to elderly people. I remember my mother-in-law's pleasure with the show of respect and support showed to her in public, commonly seen in Korea but so rare in France today.

The second aspect emanating from the same concept is the respect for hierarchy inside companies and in society in general. I will discuss this in more detail when I get into my experience with Korea First Bank with its many positive but some strangely negative effects.

The Koreans also have a difficult relationship with money, considered both as secondary and not a subject to be discussed. Foreigners can feel very secure in Korea, and forgetting ones' wallet somewhere is never a problem. It will usually be found where you left it, or it will be returned to you untouched.

Another consequence of these traditions is the clear superiority of the male. Women in Korea often have a PhD, but as yet cannot break the (very low) glass ceiling or even talk about it. Until 2005, they actually did not have an identity of their own, the identity being based on the tablets—a male genealogic history. Women were accounted for in their father's tablets before being suppressed and written into their husband's, and they would disappear in case of death of the husband or in very rare cases of divorce. The best scenario would be to have a son and to be written into her son's tablets. This is not anecdotal; it is changing, but very slowly and of course among the younger generation only. Marriages are still often arranged, and women transfer the respect previously shown to their parents to their husband and his parents. Even in the office this other hierarchy is very visible.

Like many Asians, Koreans give a very high importance to face, the image they project in society, and everybody is very attentive to not losing face in public. That makes work relations much nicer on the surface but also, as we will see, makes management much more complicated.

Education has always been very important in Korea for males. Traditionally, the erudite status was the ideal to reach. Today that means having ones' children going to the best kindergarten, to the best high school, in order to enter the best university. Nowadays, with fewer children, education also becomes a priority for girls, who often achieve top grades in the best universities, but without getting comparable career opportunities, they are frustratingly underemployed.

Success and face…

 The result has been and continues to be an extraordinarily competitive life for children and teenagers, both boys and girls, with an astronomical cost of extra lessons, evaluated nationwide at an amount higher than the total budget of the national education in all schools and universities combined… That means very high standards and nationwide a very high education level, but also despair for the ones unable to compete in this race.

Relationships become quite complicated. There is an age hierarchy, education hierarchy, social hierarchy, and finally rank in the company. People tend to stay in their own circles, friends of the same age from their birth place, from the same high school or university, and finally from the same company. The only way they break through these boundaries is to get drunk together, as we will see later.

-    **A Mega-Generation Gap**

The generation gap is directly linked to the change of conditions of life between two generations. The acceleration of the application of sciences and technologies creates a bigger gap than in the previous centuries, but nowhere, I believe, is this gap as large as in Korea.

The strength of the ancestral traditions; the isolation until some twenty years ago; the explosion of new technologies (especially electronics and communication), and perhaps even more the total change of conditions of life between fifty years ago and today (between subsistence-focused life and developed country lifestyle), make the twenty-year-old Korean young adult different and naturally at odds with his fifty-year-old father.

The father's memories are of struggling to survive when he was young; the problems of today's youth are more akin to getting the latest model cell phone or the fastest computer with all the gadgets. This disparity creates a lot of challenges. The father's life revolves around work—any work. Is it going to be the same thing for the twenty-year-old?

During the previous generation's youth, Korea was recovering from the war with terrible destruction and only an armistice. Today, in spite of random bursts of violence from the North, the armistice is more and more being considered by the younger generation as a state of peace, and the danger has been, for them, fabricated by their parents or by the Americans.

The relationship between male and female is also changing. The younger generation has been exposed to other civilizations and cultures by television, the Internet, education, and overseas travel. They are developing more natural relationships and increasingly want to choose their own spouse. Later marriages and even divorce are less taboo today.

The desire to be happy—the starting point for individualism—is at odds with the traditional ways of devotion to their elders and the sense of duty to family, friends, company, and country.

Naturally, this evolution is not as fast and prevalent as I have indicated here, and it will take a long time, if ever, until individualism, as seen in developed countries, totally overcomes the strong Korean traditions. Nevertheless, the gap between the generations is already quite staggering, and its consequences are appearing on the political and economical scenes.

Respect for elders has natural consequences. Leaders still needed to be older. It was only at the 2004 presidential election that a younger outsider was elected after an Internet-based campaign oriented toward the younger generation. This demonstrated both the generation gap and the breadth of the new electorate.

This revolution brought up many new issues common in the western world. Environmental issues were raised more vigorously, and gender problems were for the first time actually discussed.

This new young majority looked very differently at the large industrial groups (the *chaebols)* that we will discuss later. The younger generation did not feel the obligation to these industrial groups that pioneered the rapid growth and success in the economy. They replaced this obligation with hate, forgetting the chaebols' extraordinary role in Korea's development. They forgot about the huge role played in employment and trade. They focused attention only on their power, their wealth, their paternalism, and their internationalist strategies, pushing through some needed anti-trust regulations, but somewhat lopsidedly.

Every Korea male is subject to a compulsory military service, for about two years, which usually increases social cohesion and increases equality but can help develop anti-military feelings and an irrational "peace-now" approach for a few.

Consequences for Foreigners

Korea has one of the most homogeneous populations with its own history, language, and traditions that never quite mixed with any other cultures. Hence, foreigners are immediately spotted.

Throughout their long history, the attitude toward foreigners has been somewhat hostile. This can be explained when one looks at the nearest foreigners who entered Korea, namely the Mongols, the Japanese, and the Chinese, with others being generally kept away by distance. Even contacts with some European countries, even if somehow limited, turned often into small conflicts.

For the large majority of Koreans, up to the Korean War, foreigners were only Chinese or Japanese. The Chinese were like big brothers for whom the Koreans had mixed feelings. The difference in size naturally created an inferiority complex and suspicion.. The Japanese were hated as is easily explainable by the destruction, the killing, and the raiding and pillaging inflicted on Korea over centuries, ending with more than fifty years of very rough occupation. For most Koreans that created nationalistic feelings and the strong conviction that the best strategy for Korea was to keep foreigners out.

With the onset of the Korean War, China and the communists in the north of Korea became the enemy. The war effectively split into two the country as well as families. The United States and other western nations took the position of a big brother. They had beaten the Japanese during the Second World War and in doing so liberated Korea.

Following the armistice, the process of economic development began and with it, the need for energy, raw materials, and most of all, capital. For the first time, Korea had to understand foreign relations, even if its ancestral wisdom kept it as the hermit kingdom. And that is the basis of the current relations of Koreans with foreigners. Most of them are courteous but suspicious, and some are viscerally opposed to any foreign influence in Korean business.

When this is applied to modern economic relations, it develops into schizophrenia: Exports are vital, but imports are bad by essence because they are foreign. Foreign Direct Investment (FDI) is needed, and administrations were created in order to attract it, but at the same time, the public and the media were blasting the investments that the government succeeded in attracting. Even worse, the most classic shareholder right becomes a national subject when it involves a foreign investor with a Korean asset.

This mixture of nationalism and tradition against the objective need for foreign investment and trade makes for an interesting cocktail, the effects of which I saw from a front row seat while leading Korea First Bank.

Korea's Recent Socioeconomic History

Following the end of the active war with the North, a strong military government managed the development of the new Republic of Korea. Korea was managed like a corporation; it was the origin of what was called *Korea Inc.*

We are first going to look at the model created after the Korean War which only had to change after the 1997 crisis. This model was easy to understand and was the most efficient in developing the country at that time. This is especially true when we take into consideration the absence of capital and the very low level of GDP per capita ($100 in 1963). Banks were instructed to gather deposits from individuals to be used exclusively for industry to build factories focused on exports. Risk ratios and risk concentration were not the priority.

The government created or supported the creation of industrial groups around individual entrepreneurs. These entrepreneurs had very little capital, and their growth was mostly financed through borrowing from the general public and the banks. They became known as the chaebols. These diversified groups, very similar in design to the Japanese trading companies, grew very fast with a very limited capital base but unlimited capacity to borrow (thanks to the government edict and support). Later, when the growth was so important that they needed to increase their capital in Korea or on the international markets, they built an intricate web of companies with cross holdings in order to keep the power in Korea and in the hands of the founder's family, even if their actual ownership was very small in percentage terms.

Even if these financial structures were important, they cannot by themselves explain the huge growth in the Korean economy. Korea is one of the very few countries that showed this kind of growth over a forty-year period. The GDP per capita in 2004 of $19,300 had grown from a mere $100 in 1963. The actual engine for this growth was fueled by an economically enlightened dictator, very gifted and hard-driving entrepreneurs, and the specific qualities of Korean workers.

Out of the Korean War emerged individuals who were very motivated and eager to succeed as a nation and used to fighting for survival. In fact, most of these people were self employed in rural or commercial activities and saw the power of industry during the Japanese occupation. The most gifted of these received the support of government financing, and expanded their activities into industrial sectors agreed in advance with the government.

The largest chaebols that have survived until now include Samsung, Hyundai, LG, SK, Kumho, Hyosung, Doosan... These were created by one or a few individuals. Usually one individual took the lead in each group with the descendants still managing the group today: Lee for Samsung, Koo for LG (the Lucky and Goldstar Groups), Chung for Hyundai, and so on.

There are many stories about these groups and their founders. Mr. Chung, who created Hyundai Motor, succeeded in getting an order to build a ship in London without having any capacity to do so. Once back in Korea, from this single order he began to create a shipyard which is today Hyundai Heavy, the largest and most impressive shipyard in the world.

Some parts of the four largest groups were incredibly successful and grew rapidly. Samsung Electronics, LG Electronics, Hyundai Motor, and SK Telecom, to name but a few, are today among the largest and most successful companies on a global scale. They represent only one company in each of these chaebols which count many hundreds of different entities ranging in areas such as services, real estate, construction, finance, insurance, and other multi-faceted businesses.

Some went through a logical evolution, like Kumho from tire manufacturing to bus-lines to airlines.. Some others had a more revolutionary reorientation. Samsung was mostly a textile company (Cheil Industry) before moving aggressively into electronics, which is today its main industry. All diversified, often too much, and all were attracted to construction, a highly speculative and profitable area, as well as to the financial sector. This was not always the right decision, as we will see later.

The employees were also a major asset in this development. While poor, the Koreans always gave a high priority on education, and the work force was much better educated than the level of economic development would indicate. They were also physically strong (by natural selection in these tough times), highly motivated (earn money or die approach), naturally disciplined (it is a Confucian society), and exceptionally hard workers.

This mix allowed the Korean groups to grow fast, with a womb-to-tomb employment strategy. Individuals and even families were linked to a group from birth to death.

Fidelity, dedication, devotion, and serenity… the Group became the center of employee life, and careers were usually well fueled with the permanent growth strategy. People lived in apartments built by the group. They would buy group products, send their children to school with the group's help, usually have their children hired by the group, wear the group logo on their chest everyday, and enjoy retirement thanks to the group.

Looking at Korea's macro-economy is very surprising. Korea has no natural resources, no oil, and no steel, but Korea has one of the largest and most profitable steel companies in the world (Posco), is a global car manufacturer, and a global shipbuilder. All its needs in energy and raw materials have to be imported which makes exports vital.

The chaebols are responsible for most of Korea's exports, and naturally their international competitiveness is very important for the country and its currency.

Even if Korea's GDP per capita is today higher than most European countries (estimated at $19,300 in 2004), there is a major difference: in Korea, there is still little accumulated wealth coming from only thirty years of development.

So the huge investments in research, industry, and infrastructure needed for development required foreign direct investment (FDI). Even the chaebols with their preferential financing could not grow as much and as fast without FDI, and we would see that need increased after the crisis.

The social structure of the population is also peculiar. Few super-rich link to successful chaebol families or real estate magnates, with a limited upper-middle class (lawyers, middle market companies' owners) and the remainder being the large majority of the population. These are divided into two groups. One, about 25 percent of the work force, is educated and working for the large companies, mostly the chaebols. They have high salaries, good careers, social advantages thanks to the paternalist structure, and a strong organized labor. We will see that later. The other 75 percent are self employed or employees of very small mom-and-pop shops or companies. I never saw so many self employed people as I saw in Korea. They are poor, selling any service or goods often in huge traditional markets. They work seven days a week, often more than twelve hours a day, with little social protection. Often their revenues are low and highly volatile. They are the actual proletariat in Korea, but no labor organization or union is actually defending them.

This strange division of the population makes any global analysis difficult. The average GDP per capita is only a statistic, lower than the actual level of chaebol employees, but sky-high for the majority of the population.

The IMF Crisis

The crisis that hit the developing countries in 1997 was called the IMF crisis in Korea, a very unique appellation that confused the cause of the disease with the doctor trying to cure it. It showed the refusal to recognize any responsibility in this terrible crisis allegedly totally brought on by foreigners.

When the crisis occurred, Korea was overextended in order to finance its fast growth. The Korean chaebols, and most Korean companies, were over-leveraged. The only way to service their financial obligations was to continue growth indefinitely at a high pace. The crisis stopped the machine, and even worse, clients in developing countries became insolvent. This situation brought Korea Inc. to the brink of bankruptcy, with many companies becoming unable to repay their debts.

Korea was not at that time an open economy, and the government was still very active in protecting what was considered important, namely exports, jobs, and industry. The fact that a company or even a chaebol was insolvent was not enough to push it to bankruptcy, and banks were asked to continue their financial supporting for the good of the country.

As a result, it was in the banking sector where the troubles concentrated: Banks were used as tools of national policy for industrialization, and the lack of capital pushed companies to over-leveraging. In this context, banks were not able to apply any risk principles: spreading of the risks, diversification, or limiting loan size to a fraction of the bank's capital.

When companies became unable to service their debt, banks became automatically insolvent themselves. Their retail deposits were loaned to chaebols and SMEs, who were unable to reimburse or even pay interest due. This situation was aggravated further by the specialization of the banks. Each one was linked to a few chaebols as the agent bank, or what we commonly refer to as the lender of last resort.

This industrial crisis quickly became a bank crisis in Korea, and the authorities had to intervene strongly to reestablish confidence in the financial system and avoid a full-blown financial crisis. Failing to act would have destroyed the country's whole financial system.

In this context, the banks represented a huge risk for Korea. To allow a large bank to collapse would have transferred to the government and the other banks a burden close in magnitude to its total balance sheet. The state would have to reimburse the individual depositors. To avoid the contagion to other sectors of the economy, foreclosures would have to be kept very low, and the new demand for loans would have to be distributed to the remaining banks, increasing their own fragility.

Chapter 1

My First Contact with Korea and Korea First Bank

In January 2000, David Bonderman, the co-founder of TPG Capital (TPG), formerly Texas Pacific Group, and Newbridge Capital (Newbridge), a joint venture between TPG Capital and Blum and Associates, called and asked me if I would be interested in joining the board of Korea First Bank (KFB), an investment where Newbridge had just finalized the purchase of a controlling interest in late December 1999. I had known David for more than ten years, and having a very high opinion of him, I accepted. The timing was coincidentally good as I was just about to leave the vice chair at Republic National Bank of New York.

He sent me the final documentation of the acquisition, together with the plan for the KFB's turnaround. This had been prepared by Newbridge with the assistance of Bain and Co. (a very well-known strategic consultant). This type of plan is very common, primarily to support the investment decision as well as serving to orient the management team. The plan principally defined the overall strategy and the five-year goal, but also identified some of the intermediate objectives. Both Ernst & Young (E & Y), one of the major accounting firms, and Bain and Co. were intimately involved in the purchase of KFB and in the development of this strategic plan.

After reviewing the package, I was impressed with the history of KFB, its size, and potential. For a bank history, brand recognition and public image are very important. They are one of the major factors of client fidelity, and client fidelity is the basis of stable the checking and saving accounts (CASA). They are the raison d'etre of a bank network, the main value of its retail franchise, and a vital part of its liquidity. Korean clients stayed faithful to KFB in the worst of times like the French clients stayed faithful to Credit Lyonnais in the midst of its difficulties—because of the bank's long history and strong brand recognition.

I was also impressed with the structure of the deal, which contained a three-year put option on the portfolio. This protection permitted Newbridge the comfort in acquiring KFB from the Korean government with minimal due diligence of the loan portfolio, as the bank could ask the KDIC (Korea Deposit Insurance Company, the public entity that owned the previously insolvent KFB) for additional loan loss reserves on all pre-close credits judged in the new management's view as exhibiting more than the normal level of risk. This insurance policy also permitted the government to challenge the bank's demand for additional reserves by effectively purchasing these particular credits at book value.

My concern with the initial strategic plan was that I found it a little optimistic. It did not fully consider all the elements that influence bank profitability, principally market interest rate volatility. More importantly, it did not take into account the employees' low morale. The plan's writers, of course, did not know it anymore than I knew it myself at that time, but that was the main intangible problem.

The board of directors (BOD) was to meet four times a year, twice in Korea and twice in San Francisco. The first meeting appropriately was planned in Seoul in March 2000. It was my first visit to Korea. I was to attend the board meeting and two of the four committee meetings, those being the risk management and compensation committees. The other board committees were the executive and the audit committees. I needed to set aside two days for the BOD meetings, so I planned a four-day stay to start orienting myself to the local culture. I have always found it essential in fully appreciating the workings of a local company to get an idea of the local environment in which it operates, and even more so when it is a bank. Banking is always intrinsic to a country, a culture. Banking in Switzerland cannot be compared to banking in France, even less to banking in the United States or Korea.

After a sixteen-hour flight from New York, I arrived in the old Gimpo airport and from there was taken to the Shilla Hotel. Almost immediately thereafter, I was taken to KFB's headquarters, a beautiful twenty-two-story building in downtown Seoul, and to the executive floor with its depressing and dilapidated nineteenth century furnishings—my first contact with Korean corporate tradition.

I was excited to meet my fellow directors. This was a remarkably strong group of experienced executives from all fields. Among those who were intimately involved in overseeing the turnaround of KFB were David Bonderman and Richard Blum, his partner in Newbridge and an extraordinary Asia specialist.

Two other Newbridge partners with whom I would interact a lot were also members of the BOD. Weijian Shan, the fascinating Chinese-born partner based in Hong Kong, who was the head negotiator for the acquisition of KFB, a marathon negotiation of eighteen months, together with Dan Carroll, the San Francisco-based partner who coordinated with the Asia-based Newbridge operatives.

Newbridge had already handpicked a few experienced and prestigious foreign executives to participate on the BOD: Mickey Cantor, formerly the U.S. trade representative in the Clinton administration, who was very familiar with Korea; Frank Newman, former undersecretary for the treasury and retired chairman and CEO of Bankers Trust Company; Michael O'Hanlon, a Lehman Brothers managing director based in Tokyo who became the chair of the audit committee; and last but not least, Robert Barnum, who was elected non-executive chair of the board of directors. Bob had previously worked with TPG as CEO of American Savings Bank, a prior TPG investment on which the KFB investment had been modeled. The BOD vice chair was a very distinguished Korean, Chul-Su Kim. He was concurrently chairman of Sejong University and had been a member of a previous Korean government. Three other Korean nationals represented the interests of the Korean government for their 49 percent share in the bank: Mr. Park, the KDIC executive later replaced by another KDIC executive, Jong-Tae Kim; Yoon-Jae Lee, a distinguished lawyer with Kim & Chang, the premier law firm in Korea; and Professor Seong-Hwan Oh from Seoul University. The remaining BOD members represented large investors, and included my friend Tom Barrack, the senior partner of Colony Capital, and Francis Yeo, a distinguished professor from Singapore.

To lead the management team, Wil Horie had been hired as CEO just before the deal closed. Wil, while not actually a banker, had a rich experience in international and U.S. consumer finance, lately as senior executive vice president of the largest diversified finance company in the United States, Associates First Capital Corp., based in Dallas, Texas. As the plan was to transform KFB from being principally a commercial bank to a mostly retail bank, Newbridge thought he had the right experience, having built a foreign-owned finance company in Japan. He was fluent in Japanese, a language with which many Koreans had a strong but not necessarily positive relationship.

The first meeting was very colorful. The union made a lot of noise to show their opposition to the foreign acquisition and the assumed very short-term investment horizon of the foreign hedge fund that bought KFB. The CEO introduced the new management team, including two new foreign executives who were already on board. Coming in as chief operating officer was Duncan Barker, a thirty-three-year veteran of U.S. and international banking with international non-bank finance company experience who had worked closely with Horie at the Associates. Soo-Ho Lee, the new head of credit risk management, was a Canadian-Korean with a strong background in credit risk management at Bank of America. One other officer was introduced; Ranvir Dewan was the regional comptroller for Citibank, and was about to join as chief financial officer in April.

The other members of the team were Korean executives, with an average of thirty years of experience in KFB. Kwang-Woo Chang, the deputy president and chief branch officer was the only one who was fluent in English thanks to a long stay in the London branch and having previously headed up KFB's international group. Reporting to him were two executives, one in charge of middle market client relations and the other one of the large corporations.

I quickly discovered that practically all Koreans had little command of the English language, and the few who did were not comfortable in proactive discussion. The Korean mostly involved in assisting communication of the new direction to the Korean executives was the very active head of office of the president, Won-Kyu Choi, who as a Columbia University graduate was perfectly fluent in English.

The first BOD meeting mostly focused on introductions, celebrations, and first reports from the new CEO, Wil Horie. What I remember most clearly from this meeting was the Q&A with the incoming chief financial officer (CFO), Ranvir Dewan, about the bank's accounting. KFB, like most Korean banks at that time, had only cash-based accounting, no accrual accounting. That made me very nervous, as that meant that if the interest on a time deposit, for example, was only paid annually, the amount of this interest would appear as a financial cost only on the payment date. No interest expense would be reflected in the intermediate period prior to maturity, and similarly, the same applied to loan and fee income.

Being very familiar with the huge transaction volume and the mismatch between loans and deposits, I knew that we had little visibility into the actual profitability of the bank, and that each monthly or quarterly statement would be a surprise, good or bad, depending on the amount of interest paid and the amount of the interest and fees received during the relative period. We would have limited ability to draw reasonable projections from these numbers.

The incoming CFO, Mr. Dewan, was equally concerned, having come from the disciplined Citibank, and committed to rapidly convert the system to an acceptable accrual accounting basis. Accruals are the way to account for a prorated portion of revenues and expenses, and it is the only way to understand the actual profitability of a bank. I could not help wondering how Bain Consulting and Wil could have made previsions and built a plan in this context and what credibility we could give to these projections.

Very much in line with the original Bain plan, the CEO defined his strategy of developing a full retail bank, with loans and deposits, while improving penetration in the SME (small and middle-sized companies) business. This strategy was mainly based on the idea of risk diversification, where lending mostly to large conglomerates prior to the crisis caused the bank's insolvency in the first place. The CEO's experience in consumer lending seemed in sync with this strategy.

Unfortunately, as this new plan was picked up by the media, it was interpreted that KFB was no longer interested in supporting large corporations and would no longer finance the development of Korea... This apparent disengagement from the large corporate business surprised me, as well as the plan to reduce market trading risk and the related activities, but not being familiar enough with the environment it was difficult to challenge the new direction.

After the BOD meeting, I spent the next two days in Seoul, visiting and learning as much as I could. I visited Kyongbuk Palace, the National and the Folk Museums, and just walked around. Seoul and the Koreans surprised me. I discovered that most Koreans have limited or no English capability, but they are very polite and often warm and hospitable. I ate in Korean restaurants where no English menus existed, and nobody spoke English. Seoul appeared to me as a clean, very safe, but very big city with thousands of large residential buildings, office towers, and dreadful traffic jams. From the museums, I discovered the history, the arts, and the special features of this nation. Here also I was surprised. Korea discovered and used extensively printing well before Europe. Korea's autonomous history was as long as France's, but Korea was so poor thirty years ago that life expectancy was forty!

Three months later we had a meeting in San Francisco. The BOD committees were now organized, and accounting changes were already progressing. Through the information available to BOD members, I increasingly became concerned about two major challenges: insufficient growth and rate sensitivity.

Another three months later, in September, the BOD was again meeting in Seoul, and I convinced my wife to join me on this trip. It was her first visit. She was as surprised as I had been and immediately interested in this civilization of which we had little knowledge. We discovered in the National Museum both the splendor of Goryo's celadons and the dire cultural consequences of the many Japanese raids against Korea during centuries and of the long occupation of the peninsula.

BOD meetings continued to be held every three months, giving directors an increasingly better grasp of KFB's strengths and weaknesses. Management reported on the modernization and strategic progress, especially in term of operating processes, product and channel development, and new technology to support the new bank. KFB was the premier Korean bank until 1996, but after five years in virtual bankruptcy, going from one cost reduction (mainly on staff) to the next, many key professionals had been lost. Deferred maintenance was a big problem owing to a total freeze on new investment since 1996, which made most of the hardware and software obsolete. ATMs, for example, were the oldest in Korea and ready to be displayed in a museum.

Loan volumes were not growing fast enough as the development of the retail portfolio (and its recurring profitability) was too slow. Corporate loans were either rolling off without clear action to grow the portfolio or being put to the KDIC owing to unacceptable risk.

Fortunately, the credit risks were now much more tightly controlled with the implementation of a centralized credit process put in place by the new management. I regularly requested management to take measures to reduce the asset liability management (ALM) risks, a vulnerability to market rate reduction which I considered much too high. I suggested purchasing a large amount of fixed rate government bonds. It would reduce this very serious risk while taking advantage of the high market interest rates. Mr. Horie, having no experience in these matters, did not grasp the importance of this point, and nothing was done.

The BOD process Newbridge designed was quite strong; the committees were receiving reports before all the meetings and consequently were in a better-informed position to ask a lot of questions. Detailed discussions during long committee meetings followed by the committees' reports to the BOD led to very active discussion on many important subjects. Conference calls between BOD meetings were frequent, and I was impressed by the remarkable availability of all. I had during this period the privilege to know better the BOD members, to interact with them, and to build trust.

In the beginning of 2001 the CEO requested the BOD for approval to dispose of the information technology (IT) center, outsourcing most of the IT activity. What became apparent only later was the secrecy with which this project had been studied. When the IT team, the union, and the employees learned about it, they did what they usually do in these types of situations. They took it as a declaration of war, they went out on strike, and the demonstrations almost ground the bank to a standstill. Management had to step back, but that did not reestablish the employees' confidence.

At about the same time, KFB was caught in the Hynix bankruptcy with a large exposure, totally at odds with the stated strategy. Mr. Horie stepped down from his role as CEO, and subsequently left the bank. In October 2001 I was invited to become KFB's new CEO.

Naturally, before accepting I consulted with my wife and got her support to move to Seoul, only the two of us, leaving our children in the United States at the beginning of their active life. This was a difficult decision, especially in October 2001. I am sure that her short visit one year earlier played an important part in her decision.

I was nominated president and CEO at a special board meeting in San Francisco in November 2001.

My mission was clear. I needed to reassess the situation now from the inside and to move the bank more expeditiously along. The value had to grow fast to allow the exit for the shareholders, either selling to a strategic investor (an international bank) or list the stock again within a certain time frame. I knew that TPG had kept their holdings in American Savings Bank for nine years, and that the duration on the investment in KFB was not the main concern if the value of the bank was steadily growing.

KFB's History

What was to be later called *Cheil Euneng*, (the First Bank) was created in 1929 as a savings bank, one of the first in Korea. It was then converted to a full bank, growing rapidly and opening branches nationwide, including ten in what is now North Korea.

Its head office was established just in front of the National Bank of Korea in a fortress-like building. *Cheil* Building, the landmark which subsequently became too small to be the head office, remained the property of the bank and now houses a large retail branch and some centralized bank units, including the card operations.

The First Bank grew to be the principal private corporate bank and the lead bank of many chaebols such as SK, Daewoo, and Kia. In a country where everything is hierarchy, the First Bank became a symbol comparable to

JP Morgan in the 1980s in New York, the best and the most elitist, hiring only the top students from the best universities, having the largest and best clients, and pioneering all new banking techniques, including syndicated loans and project finance.

With the crisis in 1997, the First Bank, which had more loans to corporations than any other bank and whose clients were unable to pay their loan interest, ran into huge problems. To be fair, it was not the only one by far. In fact, all Korean banks became virtually bankrupt during this period, but KFB had the most exposure, and it was the most visible when it came to negotiations with the IMF.

To avoid a loss of confidence in the banking industry and a possible run on the banks, which could have been more devastating for the financial system and Korea's credibility in the global markets, the government acted decisively and courageously. Two public entities, the KDIC and Kamco, began buying nonperforming assets from the banks, and the KDIC had to take over some banks, including KFB, de facto nationalizing them.

But in the typical Korean tradition, the hunt for people to blame began. Responsibility needed to be identified. National policy naturally could not be faulted, so the blame came to rest on the executives and employees of the banks. Managers were pushed to resign or retire early, before being sued for their own personal possessions to accept responsibility for the banks' poor decision-making.

Even taking into account the crisis and its terrible human consequences, I firmly believe that the national policy that strongly encouraged the banks and companies into rapid growth by over-leveraging themselves and led to the 1997 crisis had very positive effects for Korea in general. It dramatically shifted the country from a very low level of development to the economic powerhouse it became in the mid-1990s, but this policy reached its limits when Korea's GDP rose to the $10,000 per capita level, similar to many planned economies. The crisis was a turning point, and a new, more market-oriented system was needed for the future.

The IMF, which granted a large loan to help resolve the effects of the crisis, wanted more transparent and open practices to reestablish confidence in the country and prevent a repetition of the disaster. The government decided, again courageously and against all natural Korean instincts, to put KFB up for sale.

The sale process was difficult. The civil servants in charge were doing a deal against their inclination and beliefs. This did not help. Many international buyers were afraid of the huge work and investment needed for KFB's turnaround together with all the uncertainties of working in a highly controlled and tense environment. More generally, publicly traded banks are reluctant to take a large risk of an unknown magnitude that would create a high volatility in their share price.

In late 1999, after more than eighteen months of marathon negotiations, Newbridge Capital Asia, a private equity firm, was declared the winner, buying 50.1 percent of the bank's shares for Korean won (KPW) 500 billion (about $420 million), as well as 100 percent operating and control of the BOD. KDIC (the seller on behalf of the Korean government), gave a three-year put option (we will come back on this important technical point) and kept 49.9

percent to retain the upside potential from the expected turnaround, a politically very clever feature.

On January 1, 2000, Robert Barnum was nominated non-executive chair and Wil Horie KFB's new president and chief executive officer. A few professionals were hired, and for the first time, a major Korean bank was managed by foreigners. The traumatism in public opinion was huge, and the press, reflecting the opinions of the majority, was dramatically negative, at any moment eager to show why the government had made a bad decision selling their birthright, and how foreign private equity funds were only looking for short-term profits. They continued, even five years later, to confuse hedge funds with private equity funds.

Robert Barnum, who had been the CEO at American Savings Bank, was recognized as a professional, and his function was perceived as similar to those of other chairmen at Korean banks. While not knowing how actively he (or for that matter the rest of the BOD) was involved, this did not cause a problem for the Koreans, as he was mostly chairing the BOD meetings. Boards and their meetings in the traditional sense in Korea tended not to be too involved in the running of the business.

The problem for the Koreans was in fact Wil Horie, because he was the *Ouneng Tchang*, the CEO of a Korean bank and he was not a Korean… He was an American from Hawaii with some Japanese blood. Wil, a veteran of consumer finance, had the advantage of being able to speak English and Japanese, and by this way, some Korean; the two languages having in common their roots in Chinese characters and a similar grammar. Wil quickly became the target for why the deal should not have been done. The press was continually searching for any small subject to release derogatory articles, and any positive news were totally overlooked.

Private Equity Funds

In spite of their very important role in modern economic cycles, private equity funds (PEF) were essentially unknown outside of financial circles and even more unknown, and diabolized for that, in Korea.

In my former life as CEO of Credit Lyonnais Americas, between 1989 and 1997, I had the opportunity to have a front row seat in discovering and studying PEFs and working with them too. It is important to spend few pages to explain, in general terms, who are these powerful and unknown PEFs.

The story began in the end of the 1980s when star bankers left Drexel Burnham to make investments of their own, as well as for a few private clients. The success of this formula attracted other stars to create new funds, with new investors joining to invest money with them. Today it is a booming sector with well-established rules and dominated by a dozen very big funds, most of them American.

The general partner of a PEF, usually a well-known star and his team, typically raise a fund of few hundred million dollars, or even up to a few billions (currently it can even reach up to one-shot deals of $15 billion for the largest ones). These have a theoretical life of ten years, after a three-year investment period. During this investment period, the general partner finds investment targets and invests the money, expecting to turnaround or at least bring decisive value within a three- to seven-year time horizon, after which generally selling and remitting funds to the investors with a high targeted return on those invested funds.

The general partner is compensated with a fixed annual fee and a part of the profitability created (called the promote), usually zero if the return is lower than 8 percent and around 20 percent of the return if it is higher than this floor.

Investors are kept informed, but there is no daily mark-to-market (in fact impossible for most of these investments). The general partner is the decision–maker, buying, managing, and selling. It is for this reason that the general partner has to include a star… Credibility is key to raising large funds for protracted periods on the basis of trust only. The GP has to be able to show a solid track record to attract investments and, of course, when the fund is close to be fully used, to raise another one. Investors would invest again only with the most successful funds and GPs.

In the United States during the 1990s, these funds began to play an irreplaceable role in the economic cycle. Today when a corporation is underperforming or is undervalued in the stock market, PEFs seize these opportunities to invest and increase their returns. Management could be changed eventually to do things the previous one either did not know or did not want to do, such as. merging with another company or, in the opposite way, selling off these parts that were under performing or not core activities. After a few years, the whole or parts of it could be sold to another company or could go public with an IPO.

This provides shareholders an avenue to exit their shares (even in troubled companies), as the competition between different PEF for the asset creates an actual market. PEFs also serve to finance investments in troubled corporations that might not be able to raise financing elsewhere.

In the United States, where the history of these kinds of funds is the longest, there is without doubt a trail of success, both in the acquired companies who become more successful and with the investors who get a real equity return. Some of the largest PEFs are KKR, TPG, Apollo, Blackstone, and Carlyle, to name a few. Investors generally receive annual returns well above 25 percent.

The absence of a formal and daily valuation by the market allows managers of the companies owned by a PEF to be less focused on quarterly results and dividends than typical U.S. public companies and in this way to be more focused on rebuilding or turning around the acquired entity. It allows the PEFs to take on tough turnarounds without negatively impacting investors who are really only interested in the final results of the whole fund, which of course is fairly, diversified.

Finally, it gives the economy large amounts of long term high risk taking capital, that were not easy to find even in developed economies. The original individual investors have been largely replaced by institutional investors, such as pension funds, which of course only invest a small part of their available money in PEFs, but even a small percentage of hundreds of billions is quite a large amount.

These funds expanded their reach and started investing in Europe and Asia, with some becoming true global players, usually creating in the host country a kind of love-hate relationship. Every developing country (and even the developed ones) first tries to attract their capital and their know-how. Then, finding the PEFs too aggressive, they declare them too profit-oriented or too foreign, as in Korea's case.

Chapter 2

My First Hundred Days as the CEO of KFB

After I was nominated by the BOD in San Francisco, I flew directly to Korea with Wil Horie. As the CEO was the only executive to be a member of the board, I knew that the management team was unaware of Wil's resignation and of my nomination.

What surprised me, though, was the way the first contact happened: approximately twenty officers, including the whole executive team as well as some of the Bain consultants, were waiting for Wil for a weekend strategy meeting on Cheju Island.

Upon our arrival, Wil announced his resignation and my nomination, and asked Bain to go ahead with the prepared papers. I did not know about the reasons of this meeting: it was the first shot at a reorganization of the bank that was created by Bain and was going to be discussed with the management team for the first time over that very weekend!

My first priority was still to get to know and reassure the executive team as well as the broader group of the top twenty officers. But I had also to listen to Bain's important presentation and avoid giving an opinion during this first week-end. I wanted to keep my options open to consider the different strategic alternatives.

Needless to say, the executives were more concerned with the CEO change and the ramifications of this event than in Bain's plan, and the dialogue suffered. Regardless, Bain's consultants presented their ideas with little intervention. Their proposals did provide for some anxiety, especially among the Korean members of the team.

The continuity of the team was very important, but I did not know the level of personal relationships between the officers and the departing CEO, and I could not anticipate how they were going to react to Wil's departure. Throughout the weekend, I was busy speaking with the officers, reassuring them and trying to get some information from them.

A couple of additional foreign executives had joined the management team since the first BOD meeting in March 2000. An experienced risk manager who specialized in credit cards and consumer finance, Keith Shachat (from American Express and Associates First Capital), and the IT chief, Jay Hyun from EDS, had both joined the executive committee of the bank. Four other foreign executives joined KFB as senior vice presidents, including a credit card specialist, Peter Gunton (from Amex and Mastercard), and Bill Bilsborough (from Associates) as head of noncard consumer products. Both men were reporting to the chief operating officer, Duncan Barker. The other SVP, a

Korean-American consumer risk specialist, Chan Chang (from American Express) joined as Keith Shachat's deputy. The other members of the team were local Koreans who had made their careers with the bank.

Not counting the CEO there were eight expatriates all together, and among them three were Koreans. They were a small group but all were specialists bringing a specific experience to the bank.
I was convinced of their qualifications and knew that it would take me at least a year to replace any of them. So even before knowing them well, I was hoping to keep them all as a team.

The executives in charge of the network were certainly the most interested in the plan and the most worried: K. W. Chong, the deputy president and senior Korean on the team; J. T. Kim, in charge of large corporate relations; H. Y. Shim, for the SMEs; and a new addition, W. K. Choi, who had just been promoted by Wil Horie from an essentially administrative role, head of the office of the president to executive vice president in charge of retail banking. W. K. Choi was among the few officers who knew in advance the plan being presented, and he was supportive of the proposed plan.

This was my first taste in Korean communication as I discovered that most of the Korean officers were not fluent in English and were not comfortable participating in the discussions.

I met the new head of human resources (HR), J. H. Kim. He had only been promoted to this challenging and critical role a few weeks earlier! There were a few other officers there but I did not clearly understand their roles. It did reinforce my decision to remain low key during this first weekend as CEO.

Bain's presentation was mostly focused on the separation of retail and corporate activities, moving away from the historical universal branch system to smaller retail branches while concentrating corporate activity into fewer branches staffed with trained specialists, though more remote from the actual clients. Simultaneously, many consumer back office functions were to be centralized, with all processes reviewed and improved, freeing many branch employees for marketing and client service.

For the employees, this would result in physically moving more than twenty-five hundred people within Korea, often far away, while eliminating about five hundred personnel. This would clearly be a major and highly sensitive event, still unknown inside the bank.

This plan was not revolutionary in terms of bank reorganization. Most countries had gone through something very similar over the past twenty years. Having lived through this in France at the end of the 1970s where I had been in charge of a universal branch in Suresnes, a suburb of Paris, I was subsequently moved to take over a concentrated corporate branch in Levallois-Neuilly. It was an interesting experience but less fun, especially for the one staying in the smaller retail branch! I was anticipating a strong reaction from the Korean branch manager, but not yet being familiar with the Korean context, I prudently kept myself out of the discussion.

After this very dense weekend, we were back in the Seoul head office on Monday morning. External and internal communications over the changes in management took most of our time. The Korean newspapers had attacked Wil Horie so much in the past that they had to show some positive reaction to the change in CEO.

Being French, with no Japanese heritage, and having close to thirty years of banking experience helped me. A broad background in specialties, from corporate finance and trading to retail and private banking, as well as deep geographical experience in Europe, the United States, and Latin America was an added benefit that the press could no longer criticize.

Initially, the newspaper articles were prudent but positive. I had already made a point of the importance of corporate banking and that my goal was to achieve a balanced bank, between wholesale and retail. All of this was well received both externally and internally.

Wil left the bank after a few days, and I began my mandate by trying to better understand the bank from the inside out, as opposed to that of a BOD member.

Some progresses had been made, better accounting had been installed by the CFO, and we had moved the staff from occupying an entire twenty-two-story building into ten floors of modern space (in the same building), with a high level of capacity utilization. This had been achieved by the chief operating officer (COO), Duncan Barker, and his staff, that action turned the building into a net revenue generator by leasing out the balance of the building. Two floors had also been refurbished to house the management team as well as various client meeting rooms and a new

BOD room. It was a classy, modern setting, not overdone, perfectly adequate.

Knowing from a previous experience how much time can be consumed on these matters, I could not be happier that it was done.

My main concern was communication with a big C, not only in term of language but also in terms of how to reach thousands of employees to whom I could not speak directly while not even being able to grasp their priorities.

I remember vividly some events that opened my eyes.

The Executive Credit Committee (ECC) met twice weekly. The committee consisted of me as chairman, with Deputy President K. W. Chong, Duncan Barker, Ranvir Dewan, and S. H. Lee (the chief credit officer, (CCO), as committee members. At each meeting, S. H. Lee presented a few files with requests that exceeded his own credit authority. These meetings were usually attended by some of his assistants and those responsible for the respective client relationships.

Because all the credit files were in Korean, foreign executives were given a synopsis of each file in English and were thus able to discuss the various merits of the client and the proposal. Following the discussion we made a decision.

This process is relatively usual in banking practice, and the risks taken in KFB were limited and relatively simple so that the information was usually more than enough to allow a yes/no/more-info decision. Despite this, it seemed strange to me that only the CCO presented the credits and that the sell side, the relationship manager, was mute here.

At my second ECC meeting, I questioned the account officer's opinion. He was silent and S. H. answered. After the meeting S. H. Lee explained to me that the Korean officers were not comfortable speaking in English and they did not even understand my question. Clearly that also meant they did not understand anything else in this meeting! And they were leaving the meeting without even understanding the rationale behind whatever decision had been made in this or other meetings of this type!

Since the acquisition, management had pursued an objective of language training for the staff, especially the ones who had more day-to-day contact with the foreign executives and considered that everybody should speak English. While these English lessons had merits, I could not agree with this. I was still remembering the difficulties I experienced myself in New York after more than fifteen years of English lessons, and I was convinced that we should not penalize the ones having more difficulties in English as they could well be the best bankers.

So I made the decision to have an interpreter present each time there was a Korean and a non-Korean in a meeting. The Korean staff was supposed to understand every word said in any meeting and give their opinion, in their own language if they felt more comfortable. This decision which was natural to me echoed strongly through the Bank. At last, somebody who understood the Koreans' feelings and minded their opinions!

The second event was more dramatic. A few days later, one of our best branch managers suffered a heart attack and passed away in the street on his way back from a client call. I spoke with J. H. Kim (the head of human resources), and he suggested I attend the funeral reception, explaining how these work in Korea. A specially designated room in the hospital is beautifully prepared. This is where the family receives condolences from everyone. In front is the picture of the deceased, surrounded by white candles and flowers. Each visitor brings in one more white flower. It is very dignified. People offer as well some cash which is usually given in an envelope to help defray costs.

On the way to the hospital, I asked J. H. about the bank's responsibility to the deceased and his family and how much we would normally provide. J. H. answered that we would only provide, as the law prescribed, a small amount (perhaps half the monthly salary), but when the labor department decided, usually six to nine months later, that death actually occurred during normal work hours, we would receive from the labor ministry the equivalent of six months' salary to give to the family of the deceased.

My answer was instinctive. Why should we wait? He died during working hours; we should pay the family the six months salary and get reimbursed later from the ministry. This seemed very generous to him as no other bank in Korea had ever done this. We did it, and while after a few weeks I forgot about it, the employees did not. Everybody heard about it, and many thanked me for this gesture even years afterward.

Like the translator decision, this modest support to a grieving family was taken by the employees as a demonstration of my respect and concern for their well-being. I did not understand this until much later.

I was also becoming aware of the extreme personalization of the relation of the Korean with the CEO: It was a paternal relationship, very emotional. I understood, or more precisely, felt that it was important that I personally speak as often as possible to as many employees as possible.

This direct contact was important for me, and I was then sure also for them: It was important that they understand my convictions and my goals. As I had to have a translator. I could not afford any other interface or my message would have been actually lost in translation.

I decided there that I would speak often in front of all officers (about six hundred people) and directly to all employees every month using the internal broadcast system for the message as well as the direct connection.

Another turning point for me was when J. H. attempted to explain to me the Korean labor laws and the labor relations in the bank. "In Korea the labor laws are very protective of the employees; no lay-off is possible. Every detail of the relationship between management and employees is embodied in the collective bargaining agreement, which when an individual agreement is signed between the CEO and the union, it is added to the body of collective bargaining agreement and becomes as strong as law. The unions are very strong, and they want to participate in all decision-making processes. They negotiate salary increases with the management for all employees."

It took me at least a month to fully appreciate these very true assertions, and what I saw was vital for my understanding of the employees and their reactions. Coming from France, I was pretty well-trained in labor relations, but even then, one should first learn the rules.

Because of a failure in communication between Wil and the union over the planned IT outsourcing project, I was beginning to understand why the bank's new loan production was practically nil. Both the employees and the union thought they had been betrayed by the CEO with this project.

This standstill was very worrying. Banks have millions of clients and millions of loans and deposits. As a result, there is always turnover, both with clients paying off, moving, and even passing away. The only way to maintain and grow a portfolio is to continually produce new clients and new operations. A six-month standstill meant a net reduction in the bank's client base and earning assets and an urgent need for a strong jump-start.

The fallout from the failed outsourcing project was so bad that the unions amassed huge leverage over the CEO, eventually gaining from him during the summer a list of concessions that I (and the executive committee) unfortunately discovered only later. The change in CEO changed the deck, though, and the union was now obliged to demonstrate their strength by testing my resistance.

I fully expected this test, but it was brutal. The union asked management to step back on a minor decision (I even forgot what it was). I refused, and the big demonstration began.

It was certainly much more colorful than the French union demonstrations. About fifty union members invaded the executive floor and took up a position in front of my office. Wearing their war uniforms, black fatigues with white inscriptions together with a red band around their heads, and with drums (traditional Korean drums) big enough to make a huge noise, they started and kept going all day. I was able to close my door so the sound was reduced for me, but my poor secretary was close to being deafened by the end of the day.

I called my deputies and the head of human resources to try to understand the process and the consequences on the bank and its clients. I was worried for the bank and its clients, remembering the French union action which usually blocked the branches first. In this instance, by allowing our Korean union to demonstrate on the executive floor we were protecting the bank ! Nobody outside of this floor was inconvenienced, and everyone could get on with their normal daily routine serving the clients. To me, this was an acceptable situation. The bank was continuing to operate, and I was having my baptism with the union. In what followed, I began to also understand the personalized nature of union action against the CEO. The other executives could move around freely and eventually went home at the end of the day. I was the only one held captive.

Huge panels of angry writing (in Korean of course) covered the walls of the executive floor. I asked for a translation and was stunned by the violence of the language: they were accusing me of being a torturer. I understood that it was not intended for my reading but for the benefit of their constituents. Every hour they were sending pictures of their action in their web-site. Still, I did not like it!

So, I decided to continue to discuss but without any concession, other than staying in my office as long as they wanted to keep me there. At 9:00 PM that first evening, the union was as uncomfortable as I was, and my resistance was creating some weathering in their base. Their major issue was to avoid pushing the newcomer too much before they had a solid basis to brand me as a traitor.

At 10:00 PM that night they liberated me, but they came back the next day. But then the negotiations were over quickly, and if I was wondering about the consequences for our future relations, I would have been reassured at that moment. Just after coming to agreement on small details, each union member came to shake my hand and bow to show his respect. The CEO is regarded as the father figure (unless classified as a traitor), and even a rebellious child has to be reconciliatory, especially in Korea.

In the middle of all these events, my thoughts were also focused on Bain's proposals. I had in-depth discussions with Bain's Korea head, Bertrand Pointeau, and with Duncan Barker, J. H. Kim, and as many other people I thought might provide me with some relevant input.

I eventually concluded that the plan was half satisfying and was going to be especially negative for our relations with small SMEs, which are very numerous in Korea. They would have to be transferred to a branch farther from their business location, and I knew that it would be a big strain on our relationship. On the other hand, I knew that the bank was not moving ahead as employees were thinking more about the coming reorganization and their possible early retirements than about loan and client production.-

I was beginning to understand how traumatized KFB's employees were by the recent history of the bank, a quasi-bankruptcy, a nationalization, a succession of restrictions and staff reductions, and finally a foreign management and the IT outsourcing plan they took as a treason. I felt that waiting and spending six more months to optimize Bain's plan would be a major mistake.

So, five weeks after arriving in Korea, I went public on the internal broadcasting network and in several large meetings of employees, saying

1- that I was 100 percent behind the plan that I decided to call the Pro-Branch Project (pro for professional).
2- that I had seen its application in many countries, and that I understood the pain it would cause, because I had been a branch manager and I experienced it myself, but that it was good for the bank.
3- that I wanted the project's timetable accelerated from nine to four months, and that everything needed to be completed by March 31, 2002.
4- that it meant a staff reduction of about five hundred employees, to be achieved through two traditional ERPs (early retirement programs, the only way to lay off workers in Korea; later we will explain this strange process), one of which would occur immediately in December and the other at the end of March.
5- that these ERPs will be the last ones.
6- that everybody had to resume production immediately to reach the goals I was giving today to the bank. The goal was to reach Won 40 trillion in assets with at least Won 25 trillion in client assets,

with a 25 percent return on equity by December 2004.

The bank's assets at year-end 2001 were close to Won 25 trillion, but included only Won 11 trillions in loans to clients (and we knew that some were going to be put to KDIC), and the level of profitability was very low.

I multiplied the meetings inside the bank and with the press, repeating through translators the same points over and over again and asking any employee I met to repeat what our goals were. It became the best known thing in the bank.

Even if most of the press and some of the executives qualified it as an unreachable goal (but a good advertisement for KFB), the employees and the union took it much more seriously. It was straightforward, I was not concealing the staff reduction or the pain of moving more than two thousand employees, and it was ambitious for the Bank. It was very Korean, and they loved it. The reduction in staff was compensated by the solemn promise that it was to be the last one.

These numbers were not pulled from a hat. It was the only path I thought the bank could take, and we will see in the next chapter what the rationale was behind this ambitious goal.

The other major project for me was to revamp the executive committee and deal with some of the least positive relationship issues.

I discovered that the main problems were cultural. Wil Horie came from a consumer finance company, and his approach was far from the psychology of a traditional bank like KFB.

The consumer finance mindset is actually highly centralized. Powerful product managers and central services have the high ground on the sales offices, considered at best as one of the sale channels. This would make a branch manager the head of a sales group focusing on sale of products and reporting to multiple product heads.

This was very different from the traditional bank model still in use in Korea, where the branch manager held a lot of power and above all consideration, being a kind of local CEO deciding on loans and handling all processing and administrative functions. He was also reporting at a military like direct hierarchy.

I had been a branch manager, and I was feeling what the branch managers were without any doubt feeling from this very different culture—a lack of consideration and as if they'd been demoted.

Pro-Branch focused on stripping the corporate and SME relations out of the branches and on centralizing the non-sales oriented administrative processes to allow the branches to focus on driving up sales volume. I agreed on these principles, but I felt it was even more important then to show the branch managers a lot of consideration and respect while some of them were going to lose part of their functions. They were the actual productive chiefs in front of the clients, and their loss of morale would mean much less aggressiveness in front of the clients.

Aggravating this rift, the central product units were reporting to the COO, Duncan Barker, and mostly managed by the foreign executives who brought the new concepts. The network was, of course, managed and staffed by Koreans who were not only having difficulties with the English language but also feeling more and more that they were not recognized and more and more victimized

The nomination of W. K. Choi from the office of the president to executive vice president in charge of retail banking was the last straw for the Korean staff. Despite his capabilities, he was seen to have no experience in retail or branch systems and was widely severely judged. Some even said the only reason for his promotion was his command of the English language. Given his rapid promotion, he was quickly branded as a tool of the new management and of Wil Horie, and as such he never had a chance in his new role.

The result was a severe communication break between him and the branch managers. We could agree on actions in the executive committee, but they were getting lost in translation, and nothing was happening. The union was vehemently asking for his immediate resignation/ouster as a result.

The executive committee met every Monday morning. I chaired it, and with me were the chief operating officer, Duncan Barker; the chief financial officer, Ranvir Dewan; the chief information officer, Jay Hyun; the chief credit officer, S. H. Lee; the chief of retail risk, Keith Shachat; and the network heads, K. W. Chong, W. K. Choi, H. Y. Shim, and J. T. Kim. I soon requested the head of human resources to also attend, and we had a translator so the Korean executives who had previously been silent could participate fully.

I was convinced I needed to quickly change the network hierarchy in order to have real contact with the branches before the revolution pro-branch would bring once it was rolled out. As I would have done in New York, I asked the head of human resources to give me the files of ten possible candidates to head the retail network.

His response was a defining moment for me. "There were no personnel evaluation files, as in Korea it was very difficult to get even a limited opinion on somebody. The person would lose face, and it was impossible if the employee under evaluation was more senior (older)". Answering my next question, he told me that there was no bonus system in place in Korean banks (except for the eight executives), and that salary increases were the same for all. The only management decision besides the annual salary increase negotiations with the union involved promotions but I had even there to stay within some seniority guidelines.

This was so different from my banking experience in New York that I decided not to deal with it at that time, but rather to come back to it later.

For now the problem was how to choose an internal candidate to manage the retail network without any background evaluations. The decision to hire internally was an easy one as it would have further traumatized the employees to go outside, even in the improbable case where we could have found a suitable Korean candidate in the market. The womb-to-tomb employment tradition in Korea made market availabilities quite rare.

In all my meetings with the Korean staff, I discovered the sense of hierarchy was so strong that nobody gave any opinion after I spoke, and when there were many Koreans together in a meeting, only the most senior spoke, while the others agreed automatically. Clearly this was not an easy situation in which to identify and evaluate potential candidates.

My only choice was to have one-on-one meetings (with my interpreter) with each of the fifty possible candidates and try to form my own opinion from these meetings. J. H. Kim had told me that they would be very short meetings, as no one would really feel free to speak. In fact, the opposite occurred. Each officer unloaded everything they felt restrained from saying for so many years.
The meetings lasted ninety minutes on average. It took me six weeks to receive all fifty candidates (in addition to my regular schedule), but I learned so many things in the process and created such direct contacts that not one minute of these seventy-five hours was wasted.

Everyone gave me a lecture on the bank's situation, on the sharcholders, and on the future, adding some personal suggestions for possible development or needed reforms. One-on-one, they were difficult to stop and happy to finally have the chance to speak directly to the CEO. Most were warm, passionate, and all showed a total devotion to the bank and a strong support for my 2004 goal. I was beginning to understand what was important to our officers and what their grievances and hopes were.

In the end, I decided to choose the most passionate and strong leader I interviewed, Seung-Yeol Yang. I called him back and congratulated him on being nominated the new executive vice president in charge of retail, and when the retail branches were separated by Pro-Branch, chief of the retail network. His first reaction was great surprise. He looked at me and said through the interpreter, "I don't know if you noticed, but I don't speak any English." My response was, "Of course I noticed, but I had the feeling you were the best banker, and we have a bank, not an English cultural center, to manage. We have interpreters, and I am sure we will manage our communications."

I simultaneously accepted the retirement of K. W. Chong and J. T. Kim from their positions and nominated J. H. Kim, the head of human resources, to the executive committee. The network going forward was now managed by two executives reporting directly to me: S. Y. Yang for the retail sector and H. Y. Shim for the corporate sector.

More complex was the move of W. K. Choi that the union wanted out. He was much too young to retire, and I was not considering firing him. I thought that he could be very useful in another position that played to his strengths.

Even if I was not convinced of it, any other action against him could have been construed as both a sign of weakness with the union and a strange message: firing someone because he supported the foreign shareholder and management and spoke English.

So, I decided to create a new division that included some existing departments, such as the foreign branches and subsidiaries, and the foreign exchange and trading department and some new departments to be created such as project finance, structured finance, and real estate finance. This mix played more to his strengths, such as his experience in syndicated lending. He was more than happy with the proposition even if the number of employees reporting to him was to be reduced greatly.

The atmosphere at the executive committee meetings changed dramatically. S. Y. Yang, H. Y. Shim, and J. H. Kim were communicating in Korean, and the discussions were more active with strong exchanges occurring quite often between Duncan Barker and S. Y. Yang ... The COO was in charge of rebuilding/changing processes and procedures, and developing new products for the network. He was always trying to make improvements, changes while Yang, echoing "his people," was often fighting to maintain the way the branches were working, the "Korean way of doing.", I had to play the referee more often that I wanted. The executive committee became much livelier, if more confrontational, but Yang installed quickly his authority over the network, and the connection between the executive committee and network was repaired. That was the most important issue to me.

During this period, we had been working very hard on creating a central back office facility to accommodate the centralization that would come from the Pro-Branch project as well as the planned increase in volume in secured consumer lending, principally our new mortgage products. We called it the Customer Service Center (CSC), as its mission was to assume all the retail loan underwriting, documentation, and back office functions for secured lending; to handle all consumer (non-card related) collections; and to handle all inbound and outbound service calls. This type of facility was unheard of in Korea.

Duncan Barker's project managers and the branches worked hard to complete the separation of the retail and corporate branches and ready the CSC for opening on D-day, March 31, 2002. The CSC project leader Bill Bilsborough deserves a special mention for the implementation on time of this revolutionary concept.

With a March 15 deadline, information technology was also working very diligently on Pro-Branch and on the front-end system, the workstation that would revolutionize the branch work few months later.

On the financial side, I was very impressed by the rebuilding of the accounting department. Ranvir Dewan did it in record time, but I was not happy with the management reporting. I gave him and his team a detailed model of what I needed and thought that it would take them close to one year to produce it. I was not counting on the extraordinary efficiency of the Koreans when under clear leadership. They came through well ahead of schedule.

In term of risk management, all corporate credit authority had been removed from the branch managers when the bank was acquired. This was needed to reassess the risk appetite of the bank and to manage the put option. On the consumer side, we then decided on a massive centralization of credit authority, virtually removing all authority from the branch managers. It was a painful process, and I had to explain it many times, but it was needed.

In a society where the word no did not exist when speaking to a senior, it seemed impossible to expect a branch manager to refuse a loan to a senior by age, social class, or even ranking. How did you say no if the CFO or the CEO of an SME asks for a cash advance? They were not happy, but now had an excuse to refuse by saying that it was not their fault but the decision of the head office.

Communication

Soon after arriving in Korea, I realized that most Koreans speak only Korean. Some speak Chinese or Japanese, but very few speak English, even though many Koreans had learned English in school. I could relate; after fifteen years of English lessons in France, I was unable to speak fluently until after I had arrived and worked many months in New York.

With interpreters present at each meeting and my own poor English pronunciation, the employees relaxed. Many said they understood my slow English. My mistakes made them so comfortable that some forgot their self-consciousness and tried to answer!

For my part, I had decided to learn Korean (as did my wife), but after one year, I understood that I would never speak Korean well enough to use it in any business context. After two years I gave up knowing just enough to read, to say very basic sentences, and understand the general structure of the language.

Koreans used Chinese ideograms, though pronounced differently from the Chinese, until early in the fifteenth century. Then King Sejong decided to create a new alphabet. He invited many scholars to create an alphabet based on the Korean pronunciation. Korean writing is based on phonetics and quite easy to learn, but because it is phonetic, it creates many homonyms, and a short sentence could have many meanings and get confusing.

This alphabet was used in parallel with Chinese ideograms for centuries until the use of the Korean alphabet became mandatory. Still now many intellectuals (judges, etc.) continue to have their business cards written in Chinese. To avoid misunderstanding, many short messages are always written in Chinese (such as. congratulatory messages accompanying flowers, etc.).

In my first meeting with the Korean bank CEOs and the minister of finance, I could not find my seat. The name of our bank was written in Chinese! Often two Koreans with the same name would say, "No, it is not the same name, as it is derived from two different Chinese letters with the same pronunciation in Korean."

It was quite difficult to fit in without a basic knowledge of Chinese characters and a strong command of the Korean language, pronunciation, and cultural background, especially in the choice of the form of language.

My stay in northeastern Asia taught me the supreme importance of Chinese ideograms throughout the Asian continent. Like the Arabic numerals we use in the west they represent a precise concept, and even if the pronunciation of the character is totally different in North China, South China, Japan, and Korea, the concept stays exactly the same. In other words, they could not understand each other, but they could read the same newspaper.

The Korean language is also quite specific with its three different levels: one for speaking to a superior, another for speaking to an equal, and the third for communicating with an inferior. These three levels of language differ in the pronouns used (like in French) and are the main reason why Koreans try very hard in first meetings to know your age and your social position, so they know how to speak to you. This at times can be somewhat delicate with western women.

My wife was understandably horrified when she discovered she needed to speak to me using the very deferential form (your excellency), when I was supposed to speak to her with the third level (equivalent to the French *tu*). Needless to say that led to some interesting conversations at home.

Of additional interest, the negative does not exist in the deferential form. One has to agree, so after saying something in English, one should never ask, "Did you understand?" If the questioner is the boss, the only possible answer is yes, and it naturally does not mean anything.

These misunderstandings happened to me and to my wife a few times at the beginning. Once I left my driver at seven PM and asked him to pick me up at eight AM the day after. When I asked him if he understood, he replied yes. At ten PM I got a call from my secretary asking me if I still wanted to go out that night, because the driver had been waiting since eight PM. Another time I made the mistake of ask my secretary if a restaurant was open on the weekend. Of course her answer was yes, but it was closed. Later she found a code: when she wanted to say no, she said, "Maybe."

I quickly understood that direct, spontaneous discussion—for example, in the elevator—was impossible, and so I decided to multiply the levels of organized communication to compensate for this situation.

We held executive committee meetings every week, three hours each Monday morning, and I broadcasted on the internal bank-wide broadcasting system for half an hour early in the morning the first Tuesday of every month.

Every three months, we had a senior management meeting for the top thirty-five in the bank and a managers meeting for about six hundred officers in our auditorium. These meetings included all branch and head office managers. During these two meetings, I personally spoke for at least three hours (often four or five), explaining in detail the bank's situation with PowerPoint slides, identifying the successes and the priorities for the coming months. As you might have expected by now, we needed split screens in the auditorium, one in Korean and one in English, with my presentation translated at each sentence. All this was followed by a very new concept for Koreans: Q & A with the CEO for about an hour at the end of each presentation.

Koreans were not used to this kind of transparency, and even my deputies suggested caution with so much candid information. As forecasted, there were no spontaneous questions at the outset. But I stubbornly kept the concept, and after three or four meetings with the same format, they warmed up. They had kept notes from the previous meetings, and questions started to flow. Many even thanked me for these lessons in banking and for my transparency.

To ensure I was directly meeting all officers, I needed to also create a channel to the employees, so we revived and modified an old tradition, the young managers meetings: Thirty employees were selected every year as a representative sample from the network and head office, and every three months we had a four-hour meeting in which they were able to ask me questions. These were very interesting meetings, full of suggestions and ideas.

To ensure open discussion, I had to accept being alone with them; with my translator, of course, but without any representative from the all-powerful human resources department. I suppose that meant they had much more confidence in my openness than in human resource's.

I also participated in many training sessions at all levels: new hires, newly promoted, new branch managers, as well as ethics training, risk training, and so on. I have always enjoyed teaching, and it was another way for me to have a direct contact with the employees.

Branch visits with S. Y. Yang were multiplied throughout the country to meet branch employees and clients. All the executive committee members also adopted regions and visited branches.

These contacts had a bigger payback than I ever imagined. Real confidence was building both ways. They began to trust me more and more, and I understood them better and better, sharing their passionate attachment to the bank.

Not only did all employees know by heart the target goals for the bank for 2004, but most knew exactly how we were progressing from my quarterly presentations to the branch managers. After a few meetings and Q & A sessions they all knew the way I would react to most of the important subjects. Removing uncertainty, creating a routine and giving information, good and bad, was what created the trust.

Some Basic Bank Ratios

It is difficult to speak about a bank without using some basic accounting words and ratios. Here is a quick introduction for the uninitiated.

Banks and corporations have two important documents, a balance sheet (BS) which gives a snapshot of its financial situation on a given date, and the income statement (P/L) which describes its profitability during a certain period.

Worldwide, banks are regulated entities, and as such, they have to follow regulatory accounting while always showing an acceptable level of capital, based on nationally and internationally accepted ratios.

Banks have to be regulated. They raise money from the public, continuously taking risks which sometime are quite difficult to assess, often with immediate reward but heavy long-term consequences. A short term approach or a lack of understanding of the risks taken can make a bank fail. With direct consequences on its clients and the systemic consequences on the economy, banks being by nature are very interconnected.

The BS presents assets and liabilities. Assets are the loans granted by the bank, as well as securities purchased. Liabilities are the checking and savings accounts, time deposits, certificate of deposits, and bonds issued. Liabilities are usually lower than assets with the difference being the net value of the shareholders' equity called also "book value".

The P/L can be presented in many ways. I used net interest revenues (NIR), which is the difference between gross interest received and interest paid. By adding fees and commissions to the NIR, the bank's total revenues are derived.

The addition of staff expenses, general expenses, and depreciation adds up to the total operating expenses. The difference between the total revenues and the total operating expenses produces the operating margin, a very important number that defines the profitability of the institution before provisions and exceptional items.

Deducting the provisions for loan losses and all other provisions from the operating margin and adding (or subtracting) the exceptional revenues (or losses) will give the earnings before income tax (EBIT), the all-important profit before tax.

KFB had had huge losses in 1999 that it was able to carry forward, thus it was not required to pay any tax on profits until 2005. As a result, we paid little attention to the non-cash accounting of tax, which in Korea is very confusing, and we focused only on the EBIT.

There are some ratios that are particularly meaningful. Return on equity (ROE), before taxes in the case of KFB, is the EBIT divided by the shareholders' calculated equity. This is the best profitability ratio of all and one that everyone focuses on.

The efficiency ratio is calculated by dividing the operating expenses by the total revenues. The ratio should be as low as possible, with good retail-dominant bank usually having an efficiency ratio around 55 percent.

Client assets (mainly loans) divided by the number of employees gives a good picture of employee productivity. These assets, especially in Korea, are a bank's main source of revenue. In the specific case of KFB, this ratio was particularly meaningful because it was, at the end of 2001, by far the worse of all Korean banks.

It is also important to understand that any evolution of these amounts or ratios can be explained logically by looking at the upstream values. For example, an increase of the operating income can come from an increase of the revenues or a decrease of the expenses.

As we had to fully rebuild the bank, we first had to increase the volumes and try to improve the interest margins eventually by changing the mix of products. We also had to increase the fees while keeping the expenses as low as possible. That meant improving the client assets to employee ratio, then the operating income and the efficiency ratio, and then keeping low the provisions to improve the EBIT and the ROE.

Chapter 3

How to Turn Around the Bank

While adjusting to Korea and gaining a better understanding of human relations there, my main focus was to review and redefine the strategy for turning around the bank. I was not wholly convinced by the existing plan, put together prior to the acquisition with Bain's assistance. It was two years old, and it needed close scrutiny, as reality is often different when seen from the inside.

Since the beginning of the 1997 crisis, KFB had lost about 75 percent of its client loan assets mostly by selling or putting them to the KDIC or Kamco. In counterparty, only a 40 percent reduction in staff with a drop of 25 percent in general expenses had occurred. All this caused considerable structural disequilibrium.

Newbridge had recapitalized the bank at acquisition, and Won 1.5 trillion in shareholders equity was available to support a larger balance sheet than the current Won 25 trillion in total assets. Customarily, with low risk assets, banks can operate comfortably with a capital to total (not weighted) assets ratio of 4 percent. This meant the capital could support approximately Won 40 trillion in total assets, a good starting point from my perspective, especially as most of our competitors were operating with a very low 3 percent capital ratio.

I concluded there were only two ways to reach acceptable profitability. One approach was to cut staffing by about 50 percent from current levels while reducing branch numbers and general costs similarly and reducing capital in proportion. Clearly this would have been a defensive strategy, which was not what our shareholders had in mind. The alternative was to maintain capital levels while putting renewed emphasis on growing client loan assets to rapidly utilize the infrastructure's capacity and throw off an acceptable return for the capital invested.

As I said previously, there were glaring flaws to the first approach. A reduction in capital would not be good for the shareholders. Any upside would be limited to the residual, and any reduction in the infrastructure would negatively impact economies of scale and our ability to compete against much bigger local banks. I was convinced more staff reduction (particularly in the KFB context) with an already traumatized staff would be disastrous. Union disruption and the resultant demoralization would be bad for the bank. On top of everything, we needed to invest large amounts to just catch up in term of IT infrastructure.

The decision was easy. We needed to increase earning assets and define a plan to reach acceptable profitability in a defined period of time, two to four years.

Having a strong treasury background, I first looked at the liabilities where I saw the proportion of checking, savings, and MMDA retail balances divided by total liabilities at a much higher level than is usual in the industry. KFB was under leveraged, because the pressure on the bank to raise more deposits simply did not exist as asset levels were too low. This type of structure was positive for profitability as checking and saving deposits are less costly in terms of interest paid. But it required higher operational costs through branch operations and left open the possibility of being more aggressive in term of term deposits.

On the negative side, this deposit structure was vulnerable to market interest rate reductions. Savings deposits become less profitable when rates drop, especially in Korea where loan assets were mostly floating adjustable rates.

Moving to the asset side of the balance sheet I saw considerable vulnerability. Client assets, which included all loans and other credits to non-financial clients, amounted to only Won 10 trillion, and Won 9 trillion of the remaining interest earning assets were very vulnerable. KDIC bonds resulting from loans bought by or put to the KDIC amounted to Won 5 trillion of this, and Won 4 trillion was in bulk loans representing wholesale recourse financing of non-bank financial institutions' portfolios.

The KDIC bonds were to be fully reimbursed by December 2002 and had some strange features, the main one being that the interest rate was based on our average cost of funds. This meant we were giving away part of our low cost core deposit benefits but not the associated operating costs, and the apparent margin added on this cost of funds on these securities declined over time. It was good in 2000, reduced in 2001, and close to zero in 2002, a disaster in terms of return for the bank.

The bulk loans were mostly a way to finance the credit card companies, with a collateral on their client-receivables.

These loans had a weak protection but were done in 2001 to compensate temporarily the lack of assets. I was in favor of exiting this activity as soon as practically possible, and the majority of the members of the executive credit committee and the BOD agreed.

We not only needed to grow client loan assets, but also needed to replace Won 9 trillion in other earning assets that were shortly to mature, and of course, we had to do it prudently and safely.

The client assets (Won 10 trillion) were well distributed among large corporate, SME, and retail customers. I knew some loans to large corporations and SME would have to be sold or put to KDIC under the put option agreement, and most of the retail loans were one-year lines of credit. We did not like these loans. Some had securities as collateral and some were unsecured, but most had unusual features for the normal banker. They had no defined purpose and no scheduled payments other than a bullet payment at maturity (usually one year).

This type of feature prevents a lender from discovering any possible payment problems prior to maturity. Koreans were accustomed to automatically renewing the credit line at maturity, with some capitalizing interest due, and some of these had been on the bank books for ten to fifteen years. S. H. Lee, our CCO, was attempting to transform these into amortizing loans, so we obviously needed to find other ways to grow our retail assets.

From the acquisition in 2000, new loan products were developed and introduced to transform the bank to more of a retail institution. Long-term mortgages similar to those seen in other countries were introduced together with a classic amortizing type of unsecured loan for individuals.

The Korean market had not yet been dis-intermediated with the development of a local capital market, and bank loans represented the lion's share of financing for the economy. Together with deposit balances, these were the major revenue generators for banks in Korea.

Finally, I knew that the expenses would continue to grow. The salary increases were already decided for the next two years, and we had to invest a lot in IT, in the branches, and in the ATM. The reorganization also had a cost, and there was general inflation on maintenance.

I made a quick simulation with the costs growing by 5 percent a year and the margins kept unchanged. To reach an acceptable level of profit we had to double the client assets in addition to replacing the Won 9 billion of other assets to be reimbursed in 2002!

Given these issues, I created what I believed to be the needed, a four-year asset growth plan. It was a top-down plan defining goals on three years that we had to reach to survive. The ways to actually do it were to be defined afterward by associating in the process all departments.

1/1/2002	original Plan					
Trillions Wons	**2000**	**f 2001**	**P2002**	**P2003**	**P2004**	**P2005**
Large corporate	3.5	3	3.2	4	4.6	5
S M E	2.8	3.3	3.8	4.7	5.4	6
Retail	2.4	4.5	9.8	14	18	22
Sub client-Total assets	**8.7**	**10.8**	**16.8**	**22.7**	**28**	**33**
%		*0.24*	*0.56*	*0.35*	*0.23*	*0.18*
KDIC bonds	5.9	4.5	0	0	0	0
Bulk loans	3.2	4.1	2.3	1.3	0	0
other assets	6.4	5.5	5.7	5.5	5.5	5.5
Total assets	**24.2**	**24.9**	**24.8**	**29.5**	**33.5**	**38.5**
%		*0.03*	*0*	*0.19*	*0.14*	*0.15*
Total assets targeted	24.2	24.9	32	38	42	44.3
%		*0.03*	*0.29*	*0.19*	*0.11*	*0.05*
To inv est for li quidity			**7.2**	**8.5**	**8.5**	**5.8**

Even if client assets grew by Won 6 trillion a year from 2002 (an optimistic goal), with the growing operating expenses we would not be able to offset the maturing KDIC bonds nor make the careful exit from bulk loan lending and reach an acceptable return on equity before the end of 2004.

But I was quite happy of this three year time frame. It was long enough to be a goal for the employees and to let us reform the structures and change the way the bank worked while not so long that it would discourage our board and our shareholders.

Even considering no changes in staff count, but taking into account new investments needed, particularly in IT, and the internal inflation for both salaries, pensions, and general expenses, I evaluated annual costs would grow regardless at a rate higher than 5 percent. That was the main factor to define the slope of the assets growth.

To reach our asset goals and assure the bank had an acceptable liquidity (within capital constraints), we would have to invest in risk-free non-client assets (government securities, etc.) in large amounts, and these would need to grow until the end of 2004, when our loan asset origination would catch up with our infrastructure and our liquidity targets.

So the basis of the new strategy was
- to increase client-assets annually by about Won 6 trillion without any increase of staff,
- to reach total assets of Won 40 trillion, with a minimum of Won 25 trillion of client loan assets by December 2004.

I was convinced that this kind of growth, additional investments, yet to be defined, and a strong expense discipline would bring us to an acceptable level of return on equity (before tax) that I defined as close to 25 percent by year end 2004, still on the hypothesis of stable NIR for KFB which meant stable market rates in Korea).

The total assets target was less important, and I added it only because I knew that it was important for KFB's officers. Banks in Korea were compared by total assets, and it was the figure that bank officers knew the best and represented for them the standing of the bank.

How will we find a way to safely grow our client assets in a congested and highly competitive market? Only one area seemed possible for a prudent but exponential growth in Korea: residential mortgage lending.

We are not here speaking of subprime lending but of traditional mortgage with a large equity coming for savings... and the collateral was made stronger by the shortage of the offer.

The housing market was growing rapidly, but mortgages offered by our competitors were limited to three-year adjustable rate mortgages. Here we could have a competitive advantage.
We were able to propose the whole range of products existing in the United States that the foreign executives knew well. These new products were already ready to go in the market.

The CSC would give us an industrial-quality production line capability that no other Korean bank would have. We had consumer risk specialists using the most sophisticated international techniques adapted to the local market. And we were already investing heavily in technology, both for our product capabilities as well as our front end in the branches that should among other things give us a superior mortgage origination efficiency.

The growing urbanization of Korea together with the changes in Korean society were about to ignite a construction boom. This was a growing market where we had a less than 1 percent share.

Everything had yet to be done at the branches level. Our sales people were not used to mortgages, so reorganization, training, and animation was going to be S. Y. Yang's main target.

But mortgages were not to be the only growth area. We also planned for the growth of our unsecured lending volume, but we knew this would be much smaller and more complicated given the very young credit bureau in Korea, which was giving data not yet comprehensive or reliable. The market was not yet primed for any fee-oriented businesses, but private banking presented opportunities for a new activity as Koreans' personal wealth was growing. The bank's image, which had been badly damaged during the crisis and subsequent to the sale, had first to improve.

In the corporate business, both S. H. Lee and I were not keen on lending large amounts to SME. These companies typically did not have any official accounting and no auditors. While the risks were not concentrated, they seemed higher than those a centrally-controlled large corporate action would create, and I knew that the Pro-Branch organization would not help with the SMEs. I decided not to make of this business a priority and wait to reconsider it after a strong training program and some reforms at Pro-Branch, so not before eighteen months or two years.

The BOD was still very sensitive to the impact the 1997 crisis had on the large corporate loan portfolio and was very restrictive on corporate client exposures. They had fixed very low house limits per client (much less than the legal lending limit in Korea). These limits made sense, and I would have supported them in a large market like the United States, but they quickly became very restrictive for the Korean market.

There were a limited number of large companies in Korea to whom we would be ready to lend (the others being disqualified for credit risk profile), and even in the best case scenario that all these good companies borrowed up to the full amount of our house limit (improbable, as the best structured companies had little appetite for loans), the total would have been less than our growth targets for this segment.

In any case, I had already planned to revisit the levels of our house limits with the BOD. This quickly became a discussion item at the quarterly BOD meetings, and after we were able to show the quality of our risk process we were able to raise these ceilings.

But it was still not enough, and we had to find another way to develop quality assets. Structured financing was one area. Simply put, this type of financing was based on separate legal structures owning the assets to be financed with the cash flows going to reimburse the debt.

The advantages of these structures were obvious. We could protect ourselves against one of the worst Korean corporate risks, the cross support common in Korean conglomerates. A good company within a chaebol was often pushed to support a troubled one in the same group. It was also a way to create new clients in the sense of the house limit and the risk concentration with acceptable risk. Lastly, this type of financing, being more technical, commanded a much better pricing with less competition.

I had built these same activities in the United States with excellent results. Higher profitability should result, with a better market image and an opening into investment banking and its syndication fees when both the Korean market and KFB matured. We decided to go ahead and created three departments, .real estate finance, project finance, and structured finance, all reporting to W. K. Choi.

The last leg of money-making activities in a bank is trading. The local Won market, having its own arbitrage, was a significant part of our competitors' profits (when a market is still nascent, with limited number of players and liquidity the market makers can make arbitrages and make money with little risks). These revenues were totally absent in KFB because since 1997 the trading room had been totally dismantled and the BOD was completely opposed to any kind of trading risk.

If I was convinced we did not want even classic trading activities (like foreign exchange and government bond trading) before having the proper tools and controls in place, I was sure we needed some as soon as possible. So that became a priority, and when we succeeded in implementing the needed software and processes to give us online positions and daily profit and loss statements, we recreated a small trading room.

The pragmatism of this sketch of the plan to turn around KFB could surprise the reader. I will try to explain.

I am convinced there is not a single method to turn around a bank. A custom-made analysis has to be done, taking into account many quantitative and qualitative facts such as the national context and the general economic trends; the bank history and corporate culture; the morale, training, and dedication of the work force; the quality of the managers; the image of the bank and its franchise; the specific problems to be solved; the opportunities of the market at that time; and many others.

Making the goal easy to grasp and, if possible, close to the corporate culture, with a delay long enough to make changes and short enough to not make the goal theoretical, seems to me very important.

The strong diffusion of this direction should come with the construction of more detailed annual plans. In order to reach the goals these annual plans should not be top-down but made with the involvement of the largest possible number of people, so everybody has the feeling they own the goal.

Of course, after that the direction should never change, and all successes or challenges should be presented as steps in reaching the overall goal.

2002—the Turning Point

The first six months of 2002 were critical for KFB. In the first quarter, we were working against the clock on rolling out the CSC as well as the technology improvements needed to implement Pro-Branch. We were also preparing for a huge movement in staff.

In February, when the newly reorganized executive committee met and all the Pro-Branch plans were widely discussed, the network raised many objections, often rightly. Meetings were organized around the clock to resolve issues, all leading up to D-day.

When I was CEO of Credit Lyonnais Americas, I had to overcome an actual disaster, a week-long electricity shortage that kept all the staff out of our offices. That could have been very costly, even deadly, if we did not have an excellent disaster recovery plan. That made me very sensitive to this subject, which is well-known by banks. So, to protect the bank from any disaster which could stop the continuous activity of the CSC in Seoul, we decided to duplicate the site in Pusan, in the upper floors of a building we owned there. We were now planning to build and rollout two CSCs, not one. Duncan Barker, Bill Bilsborough, and a remarkable woman, S. J. Kim, along with a crew of IT experts were frontline in hitting this target.

On the IT side, Jay Hyun continued his ambitious modernization plan, catching up on years of underinvestment in our core systems while simultaneously rebuilding many processes for the Pro-Branch and other critical projects, like the branch work-station and the data warehouse that was going to give us the flexibility absolutely needed in a modern bank.

In the time of the mainframe's reign, IT specialists were doing everything, and they had to be asked for anything from a simulation to a management report. You took a queue, eventually got an answer, and if it was not exactly what was needed you went back to the queue. IT specialists were needed, feared, and frustrated by the multiple small tasks they had to do with prioritizations they could not themselves determine. The interconnected PC era changed everything. Now IT has to work on architecture, connections, core banking systems and data- warehouse.

Data-warehouse is the central data ,refreshed all the time and organized in a way that allows authorized users to get the data they need and organize it as they want on their PCs. This gives risk and marketing managers, auditors, and management reporting specialists endless possibilities to get what they need fast and to make quick changes without requiring an IT job.

While coordinating Pro-Branch, I was working closely with S. Y. Yang and Duncan Barker to increase retail loan production volumes by a target date of April, after all the personnel moves and the final ERP.

Yang energized his people, embracing the goals, and demonstrating clearly that the production plan for 2002 that had mostly been done under my predecessor's watch would have to be exceeded to be online with my three-year goal.

Residential mortgages were the focus, offering clients up to thirty-year maturities in a market where the only mortgage offered had a three-year maturity. We priced them competitively to attract client interest and offered both an adjustable rate mortgage as well as one with a fixed rate period (usually the first three years) and with floating rates thereafter. The various rate combinations were also targeted at reducing our own interest rate vulnerability.

Finally, we accelerated the process between underwriting, lien, documentation, closing, and disbursement in a market where speed was a distinct advantage. We needed to demonstrate both internally and externally that our centralization process was more efficient for everyone, especially as we were reluctant to disburse funds prior to full documentation, a discipline not generally practiced in Korea. We succeeded in reducing the cycle to eight days and planned to reduce it even more after the replacement of the branch dumb terminals with online front-end PCs (the branch workstation project).

March is a big moving month in Korea. The school year begins in March, and so many people move that month. Yang and the branches did not want to waste this important time regardless of all the personnel transfers and the ERPs.

We increased communication and sales meetings, and the sale engine brutally started. March results exceeded my expectations by far. It was a high production month, higher than any other month before it. In spite of reorganization and ERP, we were off and running.

It was no miracle but proof that, in spite of incertitude, hope and confidence in their bosses was rebuilding the employees' mindset. Over-communicated and agreed goals were getting through, and with that, hard-work and dedication (characteristic qualities of the Korean worker) were returning to KFB workforce.

Dedication and hard work were perfectly illustrated in this one example of many at the beginning of March, Jay Hyun, the CIO, asked me to visit the IT center. I had been there already but of course, I accepted, but not before asking him why now? He was quite evasive and said that I had to see for myself how the Pro-Branch project and the deadlines I defined had impacted the IT center staff. I was stupefied by what I saw... For weeks, employees had been working around the clock and weekends to deliver the projects on time. Three people had been hospitalized, including a pregnant woman, with one of them so tired that his face had convulsed. It took him months to fully recover.

The problem was so obvious. I asked everyone to join me in the auditorium, ordering them to go home for the weekend (which was at that time a day and a half). I announced a delay of two weeks in the deadlines, moving base systems to March 31 and the whole Pro-Branch project to April 15. They resisted, asking to keep the original time frame, but finally relaxed and thanked me for my consideration.

It was the first time in my life that I willingly delayed any such deadline. In France, employees would have refused the deadlines upfront and would have been on strike if the deadline had been kept. In the United States, middle management would have stopped work in advance for fear of being sued by the employees. In Korea it was quite different nobody complained or even alerted me… not even the union. It has to be noted that during this period only the low maximum overtime of about 10 hours per month was paid. There was no bonus, so money was not the motivation. It was dedication and pride in doing a job well and on time.

In April, staff transfers (twenty-five hundred of them) were executed in a quasi-military way. Employees and families moved from one part of the country to the other part, from branches to CSC or from branch to branch, and the second and last ERP went as well as it could.

Branches were reorganized with a new, leaner organization, and most of the retail branch managers were replaced with younger officers. We defined branch organizational charts and roles and responsibilities, which created close to a thousand-person sales force out of a staff of twenty-five hundred in the four hundred retail branches. This remarkable ratio was reached by reducing administrative work, changing processes in the branches, and moving workload to the two centralized utilities (the CSCs).

Mortgage production continued to grow and grow to some fifteen thousand a month. The new sales front-end PC installed in the branches at the end of the second quarter was a very efficient system: The branch sales officer inputted customer data in the computer in front of the client. Then the system, in less than one minute, checked online not only the central bank and credit bureaus black list but also the risk model built by our retail risk department together with the online national register of property values. The system automatically provided the maximum amount pre-approved and the interest rate the client would have to pay, all linked to the risk profile of the client and the property location.

The client felt that the branch sales officer was deciding everything even if the branch employee had no power to change the computer response. Three days after the application was inputted in the branch the data was verified, the lien taken, and the funds were disbursed to the customer. This was a record for fully documented loans and was only possible because after the first input, the transaction was assumed by the CSC and all liens, documentation, disbursement controls, and file management were centralized nationwide.

The success in the mortgage area pushed us to immediately revamp our unsecured personal loan products. Keith Shachat and Chan Chang had organized a retail risk department (called decision science) with close to forty young and very bright college graduates putting in place a risk system of truly global standards. He was able to develop an internal credit bureau, the first in any Korean bank, pulling together data from multiple sources. He was ready to go ahead with an unsecured product, and we went live in the second half of 2002 with the same integrated centralized decision-making process.

The corporate side of the bank was also growing, but this growth was still hidden by old poor assets leaving the bank under the put option agreement with the KDIC. We were still asking for additional reserves for old loans that we felt did not meet our risk criteria, and each time KDIC opted to buy them, thus reducing our loan assets.

We started to create the technical departments to support commercial real estate finance, acquisition finance, and some more complex structured finance operations. These were very important for the bank. To be competitive in financing complex operations demonstrated we were back in the corporate finance business. It was the only way we had to grow our corporate assets safely and profitably. I had experience with this kind of operation from my years as CEO of Credit Lyonnais Americas in New York. I wanted to develop these capabilities as soon as possible, but it was not easy to find specialists in Seoul who understood these concepts and was able to market them.

At the August 2002 BOD meeting, I was pleased and very proud of what had been accomplished in such a short period. The reorganization had been completed, the staff reduced as planned, and most importantly, the employees were back at work with production levels everywhere exceeding all my expectations. The risks taken were low and very manageable.

We were also succeeding on another front: our ratios were improving. The first one, which I called our leading indicator, was going up for the first time. Client-assets per employee, which had become too low as the balance sheet had been dramatically reduced since 1997, was now moving up from 2.6 to 4, .still lower than our competitors, but growing much faster.

But for many BOD members, the main focus was quarterly profitability, and it was for many different reasons not doing as well as they expected. In terms of profitability, 2002 was not going to be a good year. We were massively investing.

Production in 2001 had been much lower than planned, due mostly to labor opposition which essentially stopped production during most of the year. Thus, levels reached in December 2001 were much lower than forecasted in the 2002 financial plan.

Production had been much higher since March 2002, but Korean regulations obliged us to reserve for possible loan losses from the day a loan was booked at a flat percentage rate for any new credit and to account upfront for the acquisition costs in the first year of any loan, especially mortgages. These rules automatically provided an accounting loss in the first six months of any loan, especially the low margin mortgage loans. Strangely, the more we were producing, the more we were increasing our losses, at least in the short term.

While we were aggressively going after residential mortgage lending, the government became concerned that so many bank loans were flowing to individuals, and not as usual toward industry. As a result, they imposed measures to disadvantage retail banking, including an increase of the upfront reserve for possible loan losses on residential mortgages. This required us to put aside upfront a larger loan loss provision and to increase it whenever loan conditions were amended. The average reserve on our portfolio was higher than 1 percent, which was totally unreasonable, when the actual risk was evaluated not only by us but by our auditors as low as 0.1 percent.

Concurrently, market interest rates were declining sharply, and that was negatively impacting KFB's profits. Since October 2000, as a member of the BOD, I had asked management to increase its fixed rate assets by massively buying government securities while the market rate was high. I was not successful, partly because of the restrictions placed on corporate bonds by the BOD, and partly because the previous CEO, not used to manage a bank and unfamiliar with assets and liabilities management, was reluctant to invest in government securities. Unfortunately the market rates were to collapse even faster than I thought.

When I became CEO in late 2001, I pushed our treasury group to buy Won 1 trillion (about $1 billion) in government securities. We asked the BOD at the next meeting to dramatically increase these limits before even having all the tools needed to manage the trading activities in place. By mid-2002, we had bought more than Won 2 trillion in government securities. This helped the bank's profitability by generating a growing interest margin and unrealized gains in a falling interest rate environment, but unfortunately these amounts were still small compared to our long-term funding capacity. After all, we had Won 12 trillion in long term liabilities of which Won 9 trillion was in core deposit balances and Won 3 trillion in equity.

By now, with the declining market interest rate environment, the KDIC bonds (Won 5 trillion) were yielding a negative margin, another drag on our 2002 profitability.

Operating costs were continuing to grow. Salary increases (to be covered later), reorganization costs, the ERPs' compensation, the continuous investment in upgrading our technology and back office, without even considering the acquisition costs of new mortgages (proportional to the new volumes) made 2002 a very tough year.

The board's main discussion now turned to staffing. I knew the staffing levels were too large for current volumes, but I was strongly opposed to any further reduction. It was not economical and would have been a disaster. Given the high cost of an ERP, why pay three years of additional severance when volumes were increasing and we knew we would need more staff soon? It was also impossible to motivate and drive employees on my fast growth target with the constant threat of lay-offs hanging over them. Extra staffing was used as a temporary way to have more manpower to assure this needed high growth.

While profitability was not at the level of the plan, my calmness could be explained. In the complete rebuilding of a bank like KFB, improvement would first be seen in the ratio of client assets per employee, and then in the operating margin and the efficiency ratio. Only afterwards would profitability start to flow. Fortunately, the BOD was not focused on stock value every quarter, and they gave me the green light on my growth policy.

In the second half of 2002, we continued loan production and technology investments at the same speed, and we installed new treasury software called Kondor Plus.

The absence of any treasury software had made me very uncomfortable as CEO. I knew firsthand, having managed traders for many years, that without it, it was impossible to understand positions and trading profitability which means also risks.

KFB's BOD had, fortunately, been very conservative, and there were practically no positions on the books. That also meant no profitability from treasury or foreign exchange. Kondor's installation gave us desk-by-desk daily profitability, risk analysis, and management reporting (MIS) that allowed us to start these activities for us and for our clients.

The bank's revamped MIS was completed in a remarkably short timeframe. By the middle of 2002 we had a good first cut, and by September, we had one of the best MIS possible. Each month within ten working days, the executive committee was receiving a full report including not only the balance sheet and the monthly global P/L but a full explanation of these numbers with, by product, the outstanding amounts and the monthly production levels and their actual margins... That allowed the management to follow closely the trends and react quickly.

The EC was not the only recipient, each division, branch, department was also receiving its own monthly outstanding amounts and production by product, including the actual margin on each product for each unit, and all the associated costs. At last we could start focusing on the efficiency ratio, the actual profit per unit, and from where each product profit/loss was coming.

This MIS quickly changed everybody's mindset. We knew the efficiency ratio and the profit per branch, basing our unit plans on actual numbers for the first time. We finally knew which branches were the most profitable and what branches needed changes.

We now had the ability to change staffing levels, change managers, move branches, or even close those that revealed no profit potential. The same applied to products. We were able to study their margins, the distribution, and finally see the financial impact of our initiatives all on one report a few days after month end.

The diffusion of the MIS and the fact that everybody knew I was reading it carefully was the motor of the change. I did not have to make any remark to the branch managers I met. They knew that I knew. Every manager in the bank was quickly following its operating income and its efficiency ratio, a virtuous circle.

Risks, Capital Ratios, and Ratings

Huge growth in client assets was needed for the turnaround of the bank. It was, in fact, a double challenge to originate these assets quickly, but to do it prudently so as not to increase the NPLs.

We knew that any accelerated growth would usually bring more than proportionally higher risks. In our desire to originate new business we could be too accommodating or simply get other banks' turndowns. The question was how to avoid that. KFB was not yet profitable enough to accept higher risks.

For corporate loans, we had centralized all risk decision and created a scale of credit authorities within the credit risk department. The chief credit officer (CCO) had to present to the executive credit committee (ECC) all new loans of more than Won 10 billion (about $10 million), and all loan renewals larger than Won 50 billion. To avoid too much power being concentrated in the credit risk department an appeal process was put in place, so that any loan refused by the risk management department that was perceived by network management to be bankable could be appealed directly to the ECC. Very few followed this path given the strength of the hierarchy respect in Korea, but the branches got the feeling they were being supported.

S. H. Lee, the chief credit officer (CCO), had an excellent knowledge of Korean corporations and an equally good sense of risk. We agreed not to rely only on the group but to look each time at both the parent group and the subsidiary company (which was a rare approach in Korea) and, of course, at the cash flow first and the securities we could get as collateral second. In a market where large groups did not like to give any real information because they considered their name sufficient, our disciplines were not easy to apply, but we stuck to them.

That paid off. KFB avoided the largest failure to hit the industry since the crisis (SK Global). While we were the main bank for the SK Group, we had refused to continue financing SK Global, its trading company. We were not comfortable with SK Global's multiple intragroup operations, and were not able to make a clear call on its net value. We even accepted losing our lead bank position in the bank group rather than continuing to finance a company with whom we did not feel comfortable. SK Global went into bankruptcy in March 2003, and we were the only Korean bank not involved in its financing. We were not asked to swap debt for equity as the other banks were, as we had none.

The same situation happened a year later when we were the only bank to avoid the LG card disaster and the repetitive debt-to-equity swaps that followed. Each month, the central bank issued a list of new nonperforming corporate loans (NPLs) per bank, and we routinely had the first place by a margin of more than ten times less new NPLs than all the other Korean banks, even considering the relative sizes.

After analyzing why this huge difference in risk levels existed, we found that first, we were protected from the past by the put option agreement; second, we had our own decision-making process, without political or relationship pressures; third, we were not basing our decisions on the group name (name lending is quite common in Korea); and fourth, the centralization of our credit approval process protected the bank from undue external pressure to make potentially unwise decisions being placed on our local branch managers.

Finally, we had no subordinated debt or equity in our portfolio. Any amount of residual equity that we did have was small and emanated from old debt swaps. All were fully reserved and valued at zero on our balance sheet. Our competitors were routinely buying subordinated debt from other banks and were advertising their large equity holdings (presented as a way to support the nascent Korean stock market) that brought them some large profits when the equity market was up but huge, and for us unacceptable, volatility risks and some large losses when the market went down.

While we had built an excellent risk process for corporate loans, the differences with our competitors was magnified further when looking at retail risks.

Before the huge progress in IT, banks everywhere were organized with a relatively decentralized credit authority structure. It was really the only way banks could work at that time, at least with any reasonable response time for clients. Historically, loans everywhere were mostly granted to corporations. When consumer financing developed later, the natural reflex for banks was to do it within the same credit structure, ignoring differences in levels and nature of risk. Retail loans were smaller, and the branch manager's credit authority, which usually covered about 20 percent of the branch's corporate loans, was more than enough to decide on all retail loans. I myself had experienced this situation when I was the Suresnes' branch manager in the 1970s at the time when consumer credit started in France.

In Korea, it was beginning to happen. Korean bank branch managers were wildly granting consumer loans, and even worse, credit card companies were giving cards to just about anybody, as we will see. The main difference was that things happened much faster and on a much larger scale in Korea.

Gradual loan growth and smaller losses in other countries taught the banks to be careful, and they had developed the risk processes before volumes became too large. In Korea, huge growth quickly transformed the experience into a crisis. We will see later the extent of the credit card crisis and its impact on the Korean market.

At KFB, we were convinced that retail loans, especially unsecured, could not be approved by individuals in the field. Our team had seen this type of evolution in other markets and knew the pitfalls of not being very disciplined, almost cookie-cutter, with our risk policies. Complex risk criteria with very diverse situations made it difficult for a branch manager to truly understand the risks in consumer lending. Decentralization made underwriting inconsistent dependent on the aggressiveness or the conservatism of the local manager. In general, retail loans seemed too small and thus did not appear to need as much scrutiny from the branch manager as corporate loans and added to that, respect for seniors made it impossible to refuse loans to anyone of rank.

While the BOD was impatient to get moving on consumer lending, especially unsecured lending because of the attractive margins, management was cautious in not rolling out new products too aggressively before putting in place a real consumer risk system, or decision science as we called it. This is what Keith Shachat, Chan Chang, and their team developed from scratch. They put in place the algorithms with all the historic data we could find, creating a fully integrated decision process constantly fed and improved with new data and kept current in-house. We are convinced that we were the only financial institution in Korea having these essential tools. Most Korean banks did not even have one risk manager with sufficient expertise in retail lending. Their decentralized decision-making process left all credit decisions in the local branches.

We had the right risk structure from the outset, and that was one of the most important decisions we made. First, it allowed us to survive the credit card crisis relatively well, and with far less losses than all our competitors. Second, it protected us with a very low NPL ratio in our mortgage book, and that was particularly important considering the magnitude that the portfolio was to achieve.

The quality of our risk management was not only reducing our NPL costs, but it was a major element in our ratings. All banks need good ratings to be able to raise subordinated debt or even to attract large depositors, but it is vital for a bank that was, as everybody knew, bankrupt only a few years before.

International rating agencies (such as Moody's, Standard & Poors, and Fitch) were invited to visit KFB. They were impressed in the bank's turnaround, by the growth in our consumer book, and the global best practices in our processes that permitted us to return to investment grade at the end of 2002 and continue to improve all our ratings thereafter.

With these labels, we were then able to raise subordinated debt in the international markets at a price we could only dream of in 2001. Subordinated debt is needed for banks to finance their growth in assets. The Bank for International Settlements (BIS) had put in place international capital ratio guidelines, and a certain percentage of what they defined as weighted assets had to be financed by equity and/or by subordinated debt.

Because we were focused on continuous strong growth, we always had to anticipate the need for regulatory capital. We regularly raised subordinated debt and even on one occasion a hybrid tier 1 structure, a deeply subordinated instrument which banks could include in the equity for BIS ratios (tier 1). Our very low level of risk, the quality of our process, and our proven capacity to grow without increasing risk profiles were the key drivers that allowed us to raise debt and ultimately to sustain our growth trajectory.

Korea First Bank's Headquarters in Seoul

KFB's Executive Committee in 200

Quarterly Management Conference (Six Hundred
Branch Managers and Department Head)

Chapter 4

Human Resources, a Story By Itself in Korea

Human and labor relations are very peculiar in Korea and are not comparable to any other country in the world.

To put everything in perspective, we need to remember that in the 1960s, Korea was still at a subsistence level ($100 in GDP per capita in 1963), and the country was run by a dictator; enlightened certainly, but definitely dictatorial. As a result, there were no employee-oriented labor laws and no unions at that time. People were happy to find a job, especially in a large company, and equally happy to work six long days a week. Employment, very similar to Japan, was from womb-to-tomb with one company with a kind of paternalism developing in the large companies.

The unions appeared in the 1980s, quickly becoming very vocal and often violent. It was the only way to be heard by large groups and public entities. Violent demonstrations were often seen on the global news networks. During the 1990s, labor laws eventually moved toward providing more employee protection in large companies. It was obviously needed, but it then went too far, as is often the case in Korea; Especially when more than three out of every four workers were self employed or working without any protection in small companies.

When I arrived in late 2001, I quickly discovered CEOs could not lay off staff for any reason (other than for cause). The only avenue to reduce staffing was with an early retirement program (ERP), which meant offering early retirement to employees over a certain age or those stuck at the same hierarchy level for a certain number of years.

ERPs require a large payment as incentive to leave, and are negotiated with the union. Customarily, the amount is between two to three-and-a-half years of total salary on top of all contractual retirement benefits.

As one might expect, the ones who wanted to take advantage of this financial windfall were the ones the bank did not want to see leave. Management needed to convince the real targets to take the ERP, with discretion.

Two national unions were constituted in the 1980s, and branches were created in each industry. These unions tried to secure the votes of company employees and most companies in 2001 had at least one union, and all employees were automatically unionized. Those employees (which did not include company officers) elect each two years one of the in-house candidates of the two national unions. In the banking system, only one union was in place, so the employees had to choose between two or more candidates within the same union umbrella.

In each company, the union included a chairman and a group of employees voted in by the staff (in the case of

KFB, fourteen people) who would become full-time union representatives paid by the company for two years. I was used to that hidden labor cost which existed also in France, but the American board members were outraged and could not get over it.

All aspects of company life affecting the employees even remotely became the base of a collective bargaining process with the union, and all agreements when signed by the CEO and the chairman of the union became as strong as law and could not be changed without coming to a new agreement with the union. This included salary, pension, allowances of any kind, ERPs, any employee benefit, or any change in working habit, organization affecting the staff, etc. The union always needed to be involved. They also wanted to be involved in business and strategic decisions.

This led to a huge number of different types of agreements. I needed to be very familiar with all of them before entering any new negotiation.

Understanding the salary structure in the banking system was by itself quite complicated, and over the years the addition of many different allowances more or less proportional to the basic salary reduced the value of the basic salary to about a fourth of the average salary (the proportion changing with seniority and grade).

Average salaries for everybody increased automatically each year by their *Hobong* (the seniority system), about 1.6 percent, to which was added the rate of salary increase that was negotiated with the in-house union for that year. This number was then applied to all staff, except contractors who had their own rate of salary increase and the few executives who were not officially employees and got individualized treatment.

Collective bargaining is a strange ritual each year in the banking industry. First there is the opening general meeting. On one side are the CEOs of all the banks, and on the other side, the chairman of the banking industry union and all the individual bank union chairmen. Then, delegations are created, and negotiations continue for about six months with considerable tension. General meetings and marathon meetings (meetings which can last without recess for twenty hours!) are the norm.

All this was designed to achieve an agreement on a guideline increase. For example, in 2001 it was 5 percent plus x or minus x. Each bank then began its own negotiation off this base, which usually meant for each bank, a salary increase of more than 5 percent.

To survive and optimize flexibility within this tight environment, companies invented the contractor status for workers. At the beginning a contractor was an employee with a limited time contract, but after a couple of contract renewals, he or she became a long-term employee with no union protection. The unions were quick to limit the actual number of these contractors (20 percent of total employees in KFB's case) and their functions (drivers, collectors, and tellers, for example).

Retirement also presented an interesting subject. Coming from nowhere a few decades ago, unions were able to invent over the years something called progressive severance. This was not actually severance but a kind of personal retirement reserve with a very worrying calculation that obliged the employer to guarantee employees' retirement by a certain multiple of their last basic salary.

As a result, the bank kept a reserve for each employee, and the reserve was increased every year by a multiple of their basic salary, which progressed exponentially with seniority. For example, each year the bank needed to increase this reserve by twenty monthly basic salaries (equivalent to five or six months of full salary) for all employees with twenty years of employment, and in Korea to reach thirty years of employment is the norm. Worse still, the whole reserve was re-evaluated each year based on the last basic salary of the employee incorporating all salary increases and promotions.

This system was repurchased by healthy banks and cancelled by banks still linked to the government, as that had been a condition for government support. Only KFB and Shinhan Bank (for very different reasons) were still paying the progressive severance at these levels, when all other banks and companies in the market were reserving annually only one month of average salary, as per the law.

To avoid hurting the feelings of the employees no annual performance evaluations were done, and that meant there was no way to reward or differentiate individuals. Thus, there was total equality and no differentiated salary increases and no bonuses.

The results were the same increases for newly hired employees and the most senior officers, all of them negotiated at one time between the CEO and the union (the only obvious advantage being time savings for the CEO). What surprised me the most was that in spite of this system people were still working hard, mostly as a result of socio-cultural pressures which made the Korean workforce one of the most productive in the world.

As a newcomer to Korea, I went to many multinational meetings where I remember hearing one particular speaker, the CEO of an international group's Korean subsidiary, discussing the horrors of the local labor laws and the unions. After the meeting I asked him, "So you are downsizing here?" He looked at me, somewhat surprised by my question, and responded, "On the contrary, we are investing more in our facilities in spite of all these problems. Our factory here is the most productive in the whole group."

Vacation was not yet trendy in Korea. During my three-year tenure, no more than a handful of employees took any vacation at all, and they had to have very good reasons to go against the peer pressure. For security reasons, I tried to impose a minimum of one week's vacation for all (international practices require generally at least two consecutive weeks out of the office for all bank employees). This created so much protest (including from the union) that I had to step back, unthinkable in the United States and even more so in France.

When in 2003 the collective bargaining discussions reduced the work week to five days, I anticipated everybody would be happy. Quite the contrary—many did not know what to do with so much free time and returned to work. Leisure had not yet caught on.

Employees and Unions at KFB

To look at KFB specifically, one needs to first appreciate the trauma suffered by the employees. They descended dramatically from being part of the elite bank in Korea, supporting the largest conglomerates and the country's industrialization, to being the bankrupt bank, pilloried by the media as well as the authorities.

In a country where everybody identified themselves as part of their employer, it was as if the employees themselves had been indicted. Because Korean tradition obliges people to be responsible for whatever goes wrong, KFB employees became not only victims, but also responsible for the bankruptcy.

Tears, an internal video chronicling the demise of the bank, was so poignant and so powerful that it was broadcast on national TV, and it was seen by most Koreans. I saw it and had it translated to try to understand the true feelings. It showed employees in KFB uniforms apologizing to all passersby in the streets and in the subway. It showed employees destroyed by a feeling of dishonor, with some actually committing suicide. People were crying and giving all their personal valuables, their gold—including their wedding rings—to the bank and accepting everything from salary reductions to being laid –off.

It was impossible to watch this video without being deeply moved. For me, it was part of my initiation and a needed part of my understanding.

From the crisis in 1997, first the government and then my predecessor as CEO had one common strategy: reduction of staff and operating costs to the extent possible and, of course, no hiring.

That meant that when I arrived, all current full employees and most contractors had been there in 1997 and had actually lived the drama. Their reactions were forever changed by it. From then on, they experienced one ERP after another with progressively lower target ages and progressively less hope. To put this in perspective, I was fifty-two when I arrived in Korea, and I was among the twenty oldest people in the bank, and after my two ERPs among the three oldest.

Employees were staying with the bank, working purely by dedication and love for the bank, even though without hope after it was sold to what they thought was a hedge fund. Client loyalty was also stupefying. Most of them saw the video *Tears*, and they remained loyal to the bank in spite of the fast obsolescence of its practices and systems, the poor image, and the low morale, purely for the sake of the once prestigious name and for the sake of the employees.

The absence of any new investment in the period leading up to the sale to Newbridge in December 1999 quickly made software and hardware obsolete, and even our technicians were cut off from new technology. Worse still, the lack of new hires and the ERPs that targeted older and more experienced employees created a strange age pyramid. The oldest were fifty-two, and practically no full-time employee was younger than thirty-two.

This was an explosive situation, inducing among other things limited promotions to avoid becoming an army with many generals and no soldiers. Frustration occurred in the senior ranks. They were kept in subaltern positions but with high salary levels compared to the respective position thanks to the salary progression system, which was based on seniority.

As a result, I better understood their anger when they discovered late in the game the plan to outsource IT and with it the huge support that the unions then received. The unions were always there throughout the crisis, supporting the employees but accepting all the sacrifices for the bank, and now they were there to block what they considered treason.

This caused a standstill from May 2001. Production slowed dramatically, followed by protests. My predecessor was obliged to negotiate with the union from a weak position, and in July 2001 signed many agreements which were, unfortunately, legally binding to the bank, many of which only came to light to me during later negotiations.

Among them was a salary agreement which recognized that KFB was paying its employees (at equal seniority) less than the largest bank (Kookmin Bank), and that this difference had to be cured in three years. Each year from 2001 to 2003, KFB had to increase staff salaries by, at the minimum, the increase accepted by Kookmin Bank plus 1.5 percent. My flexibility in deciding salary increases was more than limited until 2004.

On this subject the union had actually won an unexpected fight. It was highly unusual to commit for three years like that, and everybody knew that if we were underpaying slightly at equal seniority, we were overpaying by function, having much more senior employees than the other banks that had continually hired new employees since 1997.

Another agreement was to create a kind of trust for employees where they could save at a particular level, and the bank would match funds (a feature similar to 401(k)s in the United States). Many banks had the same feature, but it was usually a concession given to eliminate the progressive severance that we in fact retained.

Yet another one was a casual retirement feature. Annually, at a date decided by the CEO and the union, a window of one week allowed employees who wanted to retire early to take a fixed package (eighteen to twenty-four months) on top of their retirement reserve and leave. The casual retirement program seemed too open and too expensive, but as we would see in the future, I was happy to use it as a selective way to legitimately let people go while keeping the ERP promise I had previously given.

In Korea, the relationship with the union, and particularly the chairman of the union, is very personalized and needs the direct involvement of the CEO. After various legal advices, I decided not to fight on the salaries but to focus more on two other key subjects. First was to disconnect the officers (about five hundred and fifty people out of the fifty-five hundred employees) from the union-negotiated salary discussions and to introduce for them a salary increase differentiation and a bonus based on performance. Second was the abolition of the progressive severance. Both were major projects that took me two years to achieve.

With all of this, I discovered that behind its strong language, its drums, and its violence, the union was not able to take any really radical position, because the employees would not follow anything that hurt the bank. As long as I allowed demonstrations in the head office building and especially on the executive floor, nothing would happen in the branches, and clients would not feel any negative impact. When I succeeded in convincing the employees that I was personally dedicated to the bank, putting in place ambitious goals, it was difficult for the union to oppose them.

Upon my arrival, the first union chairman (Mr. Lee) tested me but then finally let me apply the Pro-Branch project. When he left for an important elected position in the bank industry union, he was replaced by Mr. Cho, with whom relations were mostly good. Still, he refused to negotiate on the progressive severance issue and tried to derail my new policy on officer salary.

In the second half of 2002, I proposed a comprehensive system which would simplify officer remuneration, mostly into two parts. First, was a salary that would increase by 1.6 percent annually for all (a reminder of the *Hobong* that I was not able to remove), plus a percentage decided by management. To reassure employees, I guaranteed the averages, only for 2002 and 2003 (an easy commitment as long as remuneration growth had to conform with the July 2001 agreement between CEO and unions), and a discretionary bonus for each officer ranging from 0 to 15 percent of salary in the first year, increasing to 0 to 20 percent thereafter.

I proposed it directly to the union and to the five hundred fifty officers. The union was opposed in principle, but the offer was good for the officers. They would have immediately ratified it, but we legally needed union approval to change the collective labor agreements of the bank. After a marathon discussion punctuated by drums and rallies, we got it signed on December 31, 2002, and we were able to apply it from 2003.

We simultaneously introduced performance evaluations which did not judge individuals but highlighted their relative strengths, a highly diplomatic document where negatives were replaced by the omission of positives. We also added a part that was totally objective and based on the new MIS. That was easy to put in place for the four hundred officers who were in charge of branches, but more difficult for the one hundred fifty officers in head office.

For the four hundred retail branch managers, an efficient but tough system was put in place. Annually, branch managers whose results were in the lowest 10 percent (without good reasons) were replaced and usually took the next casual retirement.

Our local executives were ready to be tough using objective numbers, but they were not comfortable giving subjective opinions and fixing arbitrarily bonuses. It was not part of their culture yet. Proposals coming in were highly quantitative, and I needed to add the qualitative opinion, usually to soften or stress the principles, in line with my traditional father role in the Korean culture.

The union was refusing any discussion on the progressive severance issue, and without agreement we had no legal way to abolish it. But I had an idea. At the end of 2002, we gave the employees, as per the CEO-union agreement, Kookmin Bank's salary increase plus 1.5 percent, but we put it all as an allowance and did not increase the basic salary (which is the base for the progressive severance).

Then I announced publicly that I would no longer increase the basic salary until the progressive severance was abolished.

That created a major fight with the union, who had their election just three months later. I was sued by the union and brought to a national conciliatory committee, to whom I explained that it was my only way to force the union to sit down and negotiate. After many meetings, the NCC admitted that I had the right to do this, after I conceded that I would correct it *a posteriori* if an agreement was signed for the progressive severance in 2003.

The new union chairman, Hwan-Pil Kim, was prior to being elected, a branch employee who lived actually the Pro-Branch revolution, but he was also a strong character, intelligent, dedicated to the bank, and supportive of my goals for the bank.

He was much more active and wanted to give the union's opinion on every subject, but after hours and hours of negotiations, we began to respect and appreciate each other, and were able to discuss issues more openly through a translator. He did not feel comfortable enough in English to negotiate directly, in spite of having graduated in English literature.

It took us the full year and perhaps fifty meetings, but between Christmas and year-end 2003 we finalized an agreement abolishing the progressive severance at the end of 2003. We paid the whole reserve and some cash compensation, but we began 2004 with a new severance system based on the common rule of one month per year of service.

To achieve this we passed through many fights and two BOD meetings held in Korea in 2003 were accompanied with the rhythm of the unions' drums. I was treated with strange names during these fights, but politeness and respect returned immediately afterwards. One cannot operate in Korea without following the Korean rules of the game.

One of the important aspects of my strategy for the bank was to keep staff levels constant. This was a challenge. Each department head always had good reasons to ask for an increase of staff, and some were right to do so. But I had not only to refuse most of them. I had to constantly look for staff reductions in other areas in order to satisfy the actual need to allow growth in the units that we wanted to develop (retail risk department and structured finance, among others).

I had to put in place a highly centralized system where I was personally approving any change in departmental staffing, even when it was only a transfer between two units and even if it was accepted, in concept, in the annual profit plan.

By this process I was deciding each department headcount in a bank of fifty-five hundred employees with the very low natural turnover of less than 1 percent. The only way to introduce new blood, including specialists, was to partially replace the employees who were taking casual retirement. Even counting these departures it was less than one hundred openings a year, so the possibilities to hire were slim and had to be reserved for specialists. Excluding these few hirings, the game was mostly to optimize the use of the employees we had, and that is not an easy task in a country where employees are not evaluated.

I was convinced our early-on relative level of overstaffing could help us grow faster. There are usually two functions in a bank front line facing the client: the servicing of existing clients and the actions of developing and attracting new clients. These growth marketing actions was vital for KFB and needed a large number of dedicated employees to give us a chance in growing Won 6 trillion in new assets each year, especially when doing so fell mostly on small retail loan growth.

We needed, and in fact we had, more soldiers dedicated in developing new clients than any other bank in Korea, even the ones that were much larger than KFB.

Day-to-Day Life in Korea

Language is the first obvious difference, but the socio-cultural habits coming from history and the environment are perhaps even more important in the long run.

With our seven translators/interpreters on staff, my two secretaries, and my faithful driver understanding a little English, and with two years of Korean language lessons, I was able to work quite well with the language difference. It became natural with time to have Cecile, my interpreter, simultaneously translating what was said in all Korean meetings. I became accustomed to pausing in my speeches to let her translate, having simultaneous translation in the meetings involving both English and Korean participants, and signing documents only after having read the translation.

Life was not as easy for my wife. With only the help (and only for the time I did not need him) of Mr. Kim, our driver, her first few months in Korea were challenging. I remember during our first days her trying to find washing machine soap. At the supermarket she found dozens of plastic bags full of white powder with Korean inscriptions, but what was it? Was it salt? Sugar? Flour? Washing machine or dishwashing soap? Or what? Salespeople were no help: They spoke or understood only Korean, and when Koreans don't understand a language their way to avoid the loss of face was usually to ignore the foreigners, to act as if they did not see them at all.

Koreans wanted to protect their language against what could quickly become an invasion of more international languages such as Chinese, Japanese, and English (like France with English), so as an example, the language on all appliances was Korean. That makes their use complicated. For each machine, we had to find the brand on the Web, locate a similar model for export and with English inscriptions, print the picture, and keep it close to the machine so we knew what all the buttons meant.

In a country dominating the worldwide TV market, we had to buy an imported TV. They were the only ones giving a choice of languages.

We had a beautiful apartment overlooking the Han River in a four-floor villa, a symbol of luxury in a city full of high-rise buildings. Our only handicap was we were unable to speak directly to the guard or the super, as he spoke no English. That could be quite a problem if something abnormal happened, such as a power shortage.

Fortunately, we found a part-time housekeeper, Mrs. Yang, who spoke English fluently. She made herself irreplaceable very quickly, being both efficient and intelligent. She made our home life much easier.

After few months, we were totally installed and ready to explore on our own. One Saturday afternoon, returning from the office, I said to the driver, "See you on Monday, and leave me the car.". He tried to make me change my mind, arguing that he had free time, he would love to drive us, and so on. In fact, he had the feeling that to not drive was to not do his duty and he was worried about leaving "his" car in my hands. But I kept my position.

My wife and I decided to go by ourselves to the movies. What an adventure! First we needed to drive for the first time out of our neighborhood and across the river to the COEX complex, a very large exposition center with many movie theaters and a parking lot. It was only six miles in total, but Seoul had very few streets signs, and the use of a map was critical. We eventually reached COEX. Parking was a problem by itself, with no English signage and a lot of cars. We had to remember where we parked, and there was no way to ask for help.

Then we went to the ten movie theaters, trying to find a movie to watch. All the advertisements were in Korean, even for the foreign movies, which were all presented in the original version with Korean sub-titles. We had to guess from the pictures what a movie was and take a bet. After getting tickets, we had to find the particular theater and our seats (pre-assigned seating is always applied in Korea). After the movie, we needed to find our car in the chaos of the parking lot.

We got home happy with our newly recovered independence but actually quite exhausted. It was, of course, easier a few months later when we were able to read the Korean alphabet and guess more easily the words behind what we were reading.

We decided early on to use our stay in Korea to discover Korea, first Seoul but then the rest of the country as well. We were already culturally attracted, and we wanted to learn, to visit. There were so many places to visit in Korea, even if support for foreign tourism was yet to be built. The palaces and museums in Seoul gave us an initial flavor and some basic idea, but the soul of Korea was to be found in the traditional markets and the Buddhist temples.

Nandaemun and Dandaemun are cities within the city, in a way similar to the souks and bazaars in North Africa but much larger and selling both wholesale and retail. They are huge places where hundreds of buildings are interconnected both above and below ground and full of small shops. One floor might be selling only Christmas decorations and another one only hair accessories. Thousands of vendors sell everything from pearl necklaces worth Won 50 million (about $50,000), to paper boxes worth Won 2,000 ($2). Truly fascinating. My wife became so knowledgeable in Nandaemun that she soon felt comfortable serving as a guide!

One thing to remember in Korea is the method of counting money. It is not based on thousand increments like in the west, but rather on increments of ten thousand. We say one thousand and they say one *mann*, which led to some interesting mistakes, especially in negotiations with vendors. When one asked the price, the vendor would write or show 50 ... but was it Won 50,000 or 50 mann, which meant 50 x 10000 won or Won 500,000? More discussion was always needed before establishing the initial basis for negotiation.

More serious was the effect of the same problem in banking. A 100 loan could mean Won 100 billion ($100 million) like in any global organization, or was it 100 mann, which meant 100 x 10000 x 10000, so Won 10 billion only? Easy... when you know.

Because Korea was poor, and because the Japanese invaders burned most of the original palaces (which for many were subsequently re-built many times), the best remnants of authentic Korean architecture were some old Buddhist temples out of the main cities. Most of these temples are in beautiful settings, with mountains, rivers, and often in a large protected national park. Their size, their beauty, and their serenity are impressive, and they continue to be used in the same way as they were centuries ago.

In the Shilla capital of Kyangju, both the impressive Sokoram, with its eighth century stone Buddha statue and Bulguk-sa are the best known Buddhist temples. But each of the three largest Korean temples still in activity and scattered in the country, Tongdo-sa, Hein-sa, and Songyeng-sa, are well worth the trip, as well as the hundreds of other smaller temples, each with its own characteristics and history.

On the week-ends my wife and I made a point to visit temples everywhere, and I was also doing so each time it was possible after visits in the regional offices.

We were so fascinated by Hein-sa, for example, that we always took visiting family and friends there, ultimately visiting it five times in three years, each time discovering new wonders. Hein-sa is not only a huge and beautiful temple in a beautiful setting, but it is also one of the oldest libraries in the world. Eighty-eight thousand printing woodblocks done in the thirteenth century relating the whole Buddhist scriptures are kept in a fourteenth century building especially built at that time to combat humidity. This library, called the Trepitaka, is classified as a World Treasure by the United Nations, but it is so far from tourist track that mostly only Koreans ever visit it.

There are also large, magnificent, authentic events like Buddha's Birthday and the Lantern Parade, or *Yongsangjae*, which would have been internationally advertised like Carnival in Brazil or the religious parades of Spain, but not in Korea. Even living in Korea, often one finds out about these festivals by accident. My wife and I became "the foreigners who know Korea better than many Koreans".

Another major moment in our discovery of Korea was the World Cup of Soccer, which was hosted by Japan and Korea in 2002. Nobody actually thought that Korea would get through the first round, but when it became a possibility, the game suddenly was transformed in a manifestation of national pride, attracting hundreds of thousands of young people, all in red T-shirts. Those who were not lucky or rich enough to attend the games came to city centers to watch the game on huge screens, the largest crowd being meeting at Seoul's city hall close to our bank headquarters.

One of my best memories was on the Saturday afternoon of the quarter-finals. My wife and I went, wearing the compulsory red T-shirts, to city hall, where more than one million people had gathered. All were smiling and polite, with their children or parents or both. We never had any concern being in such a large crowd. Each goal was punctuated by a huge clamor, and at the end people were kissing each other, including us! Afterward, everyone left quietly after cleaning up their garbage. With such a huge gathering, there was surprisingly no garbage left. No paper, not even a flower pot was damaged. In a country considered in many aspects as tough and very often seen as violent, it was a lesson for all.

As the only foreigner then managing a large Korean bank, I was often quoted or interviewed, with my picture appearing in newspapers and magazines several times –a –week, and I was one of the few men in Korea to sport a beard, so I was quite well-known and very often recognized, even in my first visits to restaurants or shops. The bank logo pin on my jacket collar, a must in Korea, confirmed my ID very quickly, if needed.

Living in Seoul (after these few anecdotes) was relatively easy and far different from the horror stories told by expatriates who lived in Korea twenty years before. Keep in mind that the GDP per capita multiplied by more than five times during these twenty years.

Seoul became a clean and highly secure city with new internationally-recognized hotels, international restaurants, and excellent medical facilities, if you can break the communication barrier. The new airport at Incheon is one of the best in the world and is both efficient and harmonious.

The Seoul art scene is vibrant from traditional music and dance to contemporary painting and many Korean art shows are now reaching world wide notoriety.

But Koreans do not live like westerners. Men usually enjoy lunch and dinner together, and women tend to eat at home or in restaurants with other women. After dinner, the men very often gather in bars to drink and sing together. Drinking together is considered a social and business necessity, until the alcohol kills the tight social constraints of age, status, and university and allows more open contact. The men tend to stay in bars very late. It is widely considered as absolutely needed to develop relations, and liver disease has been accepted in Korea as a business sickness!

Fortunately the type of alcohol consumed has improved dramatically over the years, such that Korea is now one of the largest consumers of premium scotch whiskies in the world.

In front of these types of customs, I very early on made the decision that I would not socialize in this way. I would attend dinners and then leave before the serious drinking started, never recognizing that I knew anything about the bar scene. It was better for all, for my health, my family life, and even my Korean colleagues, and my participation with Cecile, my interpreter, would certainly have changed the atmosphere.

My wife and I decided to cultivate further our cultural differences by inviting local clients and their spouses into our home, just like in Paris or New York. But that was very different from Korea's usage.

It was initially difficult, but with the help of interpreters, we succeeded in making these dinners enjoyable for everyone and especially for the spouses, for whom this was, in most cases, their first and only "business" dinner in a nice apartment, furnished with Korean antiques and with an interpreter to allow them to understand and communicate with my wife.

Most spouses were highly educated, and after bridging the language difference, we had no problem at all maintaining these events.

The national dress for women in Korea is the hanbock, and it is actually worn on each important occasion. Many Korean women who came to dinner in our home wore their hanbocks.

For KFB's seventy-fifth anniversary, my colleagues asked me to wear the traditional Korean costume, the men's equivalent of the Hanbock. I thought it would have been a bit strange to be the only one in Korean traditional costume, as our Korean guests would come directly from their offices in the traditional dark suits. But I appreciated the symbolism, and I discussed it with our local executives. Finally we convinced my wife, Annie, and Elizabeth Barker, the COO's wife, to wear a hanbock (like most of the Korean women who would be present at the ceremony), and I would get a Korean traditional suit for myself, but only wear it to record a DVD of my speech that would be shown to all the employees and clients on the TV screens displayed in our branch network. It was highly appreciated.

It is difficult to speak of the day-to-day life of an executive in Korea without speaking of golf.

Korea is a mountain country with little usable space and was poor until recently. For these reasons, golf courses are scarce in Korea, especially when compared to the number of people totally golf-nuts. Golf is for all Korean executives the ultimate reward, sport, and social activity.

Golf was a very expensive sport in Korea as there was a structural disequilibrium between offer and demand. A good private club entry fee was five to ten times a yearly executive salary, and after that each run was quite costly. So, when invited, a Korean executive usually accepted with pleasure and tried hard to get the most of this rare experience. That meant being ready to play at night (some course are lit!), in freezing cold, or in rain.

Koreans being naturally and culturally perfectionist and face conscious, could not imagine being average players. Many of them practiced every day, or at least many times a week. Huge practice centers with many floors and a big net were everywhere in Seoul and open 24/7.

When the KDIC and then Newbridge took control, one of their first decisions was to sell all the executives' golf-memberships, quite understandable in this context but disastrous for the officers' morale and the marketing action.

Clients put so much on golf relations that I had to reestablish this important activity, letting the executives invite clients and even organizing contests and outings. No weekend executive seminar is thinkable without a golf competition.

When I arrived in Korea I was very much a beginner. I only played a couple of time casually in the previous years. It quickly became a major concern. My executives and especially the head of the retail network, S. Y. Yang, insisted I chair the outings we were organizing for clients, and I not only had to play but to open the game with a hundred people watching, a real nightmare.

I had to learn and improve quickly. They found me a teacher, but he only spoke Korean. I like to think it was the main reason for my limited improvement.

If my ego suffered a lot playing golf in Korea, I still keep memories of astonishing golf courses. I had the honor of being invited by Mr. Park, the head of Kumho Group, to play with him at the Asiana golf club that he owns, one of the most beautiful courses I ever saw, but he was so good a player that I was tempted to walk and not play.

In 2004, I finally dared to take a membership at Hanyang Benest, the beautiful and select club created by the founder of the Samsung Group and open only to CEOs. That gives an idea of the value to a client to be invited to play there, even with a poor partner.

KFB's External Relations

Korean schizophrenia surrounding foreign investment had many consequences on KFB relations with the media and with many civil servants and politicians.

While Korea as a country needed and was actively looking for foreign direct investments, for many the subject was to prove that foreigners would fail because of their short-term investment horizons, their greediness, and their ignorance of the Korean reality. They also wanted to prove that the government was wrong to sell KFB to foreign investors, hoping to avoid any further foreign intrusion into the local marketplace.

My predecessor was a prime target, but it was less true for me during the first few weeks. I had changed the script, saying that we would support Korea, Inc. and lend selectively to large corporations, and that we would grow rapidly. I was very cautious to avoid offending Korean pride in whatever way.

Despite this, my grace period was quite short. In the beginning of 2002, many articles appeared in the press attacking our investor, Newbridge Capital Asia (Newbridge), KFB, and its employees. This aggression was so obvious and the points so biased or plain wrong that I decided to fight back. This decision was taken not only to re-establish the truth but also to bolster employee morale. They had been very happy to no longer be the target of negative press for a short period, and these new attacks were again putting them in a defensive position in front of clients and competitors when I wanted them aggressive and focusing on gaining market share.

After discussing the issue with the executive team, I understood that the press who followed the banking industry had a permanent base on the first floor of Bank of Korea, so I decided to go there without an invitation to make my case in front of all the journalists.

I went with only my interpreter. I walked through their dozens of booths and introduced myself. The respect for hierarchy played fully, and they all stopped what they were doing to come in the meeting area where I was able to address them. I made a speech that showed both my emotion and my frustration at the bad faith of some newspapers. One by one, I gave details refuting their allegations. Then I took questions, and there were many. Finally, I told them I would return every time my frustration with inaccurate or irresponsible reporting reached an unacceptable level.

Koreans are very emotional and understand emotion, I am sure that looking at me and hearing me defend the Korean employees and a Korean company with emotion created a bond

This expedition was a success. It got a very light review in the following dailies, as expected, but the unwarranted attacks stopped and never got as nasty again. More importantly, the employees whom I had kept informed of my action through a special internal broadcast discovered that it was possible to fight back and admired my aggressiveness defending the name of KFB.

Following this, the most classic situation we had to confront was biased comparisons. Not with erroneous numbers, because numbers were readily accessible at the FSS (bank regulator in Korea) Web site... When newspapers started comparing banks by loan volume, we were in the chart as the smallest of the national banks, but when the comparison was about nonperforming assets (NPLs) or rate of growth, where we were by far the best in the market, we were forgotten and not mentioned at all.

High level relations in Korea, were mostly done by telephone with the CEO and the regulators and the press were unable to communicate with us this way as I did not speak Korean. To palliate this communication gap I officially designated the CIO, Jay Hyun, as the executive responsible for communications in addition to managing the technology, and I asked him to communicate with all the principals in the government and the press as my representative.

The situation improved greatly, but we were always vulnerable with one nasty journalist whose publisher could not stop or, worse, with one inspector representing one of our regulators who thought that his mission, his national duty, was to attack foreigners and KFB, which was becoming a symbol by itself.

This anecdote about retail risk was quite symptomatic: At the beginning of the credit card crisis in 2003, the FSS organized a specific inspection of all the Korean banks to review the ways risks on individuals were being managed. The inspectors spent a few days with our consumer risk area under Keith Shachat and left after saying that the name of the two best banks in this field would be published.

A few days later, Keith Shachat came in my office with one Korean officer from his team. The young specialist was devastated: He had called the inspector and asked him which banks would be announced as the best (sure that KFB would be one). We were the only Korean bank to have a department specializing in retail risks, but the answer from the official took him by surprise. "Kookmin Bank and Woori Bank are the best ones," and that was reported in the newspapers the following week.

That very same day, I was visiting the FSS on a totally different issue, when I was surprised to hear a high-ranking officer from this institution congratulating me for KFB's exceptionally good retail risk management. He even told me that we were the best in the market. My conclusion was obviously that the inspection team had understood the subject and arrived at the right conclusion, but it was unthinkable that in the public domain a bank managed by foreigners could be better than Korean-managed banks, whatever the subject.

I was congratulated many times, one-on-one, by the regulators or other officials, but none would repeat this in public. The only one who had this courage, and I am still very touched by his openness and transparency, was the governor of the Bank of Korea, Mr. Park Seung, who officially congratulated the KFB's achievements at our seventy-fifth anniversary reception.

Some regulator's inspectors were so opposed to us that not only what was said but also the substance of their report was biased. Their harsh reports included criticism about our risks, while we knew that we had at least ten times less non performing loans than the next Korean bank; criticism about not having derivatives trading software while refusing to take into account that we were not trading derivatives at all; and systematic under-notation in all subjective regulatory reviews.

At higher levels, this would usually be softened as the institution could not show an obvious antiforeigner stance, but it was always very difficult inside the administration to get anybody to defend us. It would have been seen by most as unpatriotic.

We got the same reaction from the Korean rating agencies. From 2003, we were rated among the best Korean banks by the international rating agencies, but not by the Korean rating agencies, who were still rating KFB lower than other Korean banks, including the ones in deep trouble like KEB and ChoHeung Bank before they were eventually sold. To publicly announce that KFB was better rated than any other Korean bank was politically simply not possible.

I also gave many lectures at universities and to professional associations. It was my way to give my opinion on delicate subjects and to defend these opinions. I quickly understood that it was the best way to get my points to the media and to the authorities. Many of my lectures were reported in the press. I have always liked teaching, but I found these lectures in Korea particularly rewarding. Students were very attentive, very receptive, and when, after being pushed, they asked questions and gave their opinions, the discussion was lively and very instructive for me. It helped me understand their opinions and beliefs on many subjects. They were often objectively wrong but faithful to their socio-cultural environment.

But the most interesting public relations saga that was not intended as such happened when it became very clear that our centralized service centers (CSCs) were a success. It was natural to recognize their head for this success. By promoting her, Duncan Barker and I decided to make of her our first female *sangmu-daewoo,* a title equivalent to senior vice president. Ms. Kim Seon Ju had earned this promotion as a tough and performance-oriented manager in the bank. We had noted some resistance to this promotion from some local executives, but we were surely not fully aware of the national effects of our decision.

Kim Seon Ju was in fact the first woman nominated at the SVP level in the whole of Korea! We were in all newspapers, and she was asked to give conferences at the leading women's universities. She became a role model for aspiring female executives for no other reason than she had performed in a traditionally male-oriented industry and been recognized for it. She deserved this recognition. At home, I got strong support from my wife, happy to see me supporting women's rights in Korea and contributing in the reduction of the glass ceiling.

Buddha's Birthday in Seoul

Buddha's Birthday Night in Seoul

Trepitaka at Heinsa (Temple)

Bulkugsa at Kyangju

Yongsanjae ritual, Seoul

Chapter 5

2003—The Year of the Credit Card Crisis

At the beginning of 2003 I was very happy of what had been achieved. We were ahead of our loan production goals with Won 18.2 trillion in client assets versus Won 16.8 trillion in my optimistic plan. Both the corporate and the retail groups were producing more than ever, more than twice the growth of the second fastest growing bank in Korea.

Our re-engineered back office was working very well, some months handling as many as fifteen thousand new retail mortgage contracts, among other things. This new capability allowed us to focus one thousand branch employees on our retail sales, one thousand employees fully dedicated to sales and client service out of our total staff of fifty-five hundred. This was a much greater proportion than any other Korean bank, perhaps even the largest absolute number of salesmen of any Korean bank,. Because we had made an early but unpopular decision to centralize many branch activities into the CSCs and decided to not reduce staff but to use it. The new merit-based officer remuneration had started, and morale was high.

The KDIC bonds were reimbursed as planned, and the fixed rate government bonds we had purchased had appreciated in value due to the continued decrease in market interest rates. The disappearance of the negative margin KDIC bonds and the strong reduction in bulk loans replaced by actual loans to clients helped our net interest margin, which increased from 2 to 2.5 percent between June 2002 and June 2003.

We went to the international market to raise subordinated debt and succeeded much better than hoped. The investors liked our story. We were growing, mostly in residential mortgages, and our nonperforming loans (NPLs) were by far the lowest of any bank in Korea.

The growth in both loan volumes and interest margins boosted our quarterly operating margin, which reached Won 91.4 billion in June 2003 versus Won 51.5 billion in the same period the previous year. The efficiency ratio (operating costs divided by total revenues) went down from 74 percent last year to 64.8 percent in the second quarter of 2003; still too high, but rapidly improving.

All these results would have been much better if falling interest rates in Korea had not negatively impacted our interest margin by more than Won 40 billion in 2003 compared to 2002, even considering our large government bond investments. The other Korean banks were not as vulnerable to falling interest rates as they had large fixed rate corporate bond portfolios, and they also had large equity holdings ostensibly to support the Korean economy and the Korean stock market. A risk policy mandated by our BOD had obliged the bank to sell its portfolio of corporate fixed rate instruments and was, of course, forbidding the bank from any stock holdings.

As good as 2003 was looking for KFB, things were about to change. In Korea, it became the year of the credit card crisis. The price of excessive growth in consumer spending and the excessive lending that supported it came home to roost.

Korea was a cash society; personal checks did not exist. For very large amounts, the only payment means were wire transfers or bank checks. (Strangely, banks were still allowed to issue checks in large amounts, which could be used like currency issued by the Central Bank.) In 2000, credit cards started to attract interest and to take some market share in Korea. Samsung and LG Groups created subsidiaries to issue credit cards, with Kookmin Card and KEB Card, the largest bank subsidiary issuers. A group of major banks had also gotten together years before to create their own issuer called BC Card. KFB was one of the investors-partners in BC Card.

But there was one major flaw in the process. These cards were not really credit cards as we know them. They were cash cards that offered cash advances with full payment expected each month.

But as with many things in Korea, cards were pushed too strongly, too fast, and with a lot of government encouragement.

The card companies, some linked to department stores, had no retail risk experience, no risk models, and basically sold or more precisely gave out plastic like a new gadget. Growth was incredible. At the end of 2003, penetration of credit cards in Korea was second only to the United States. Each Korean had on average five credit cards, and because they were basically cash cards, they were all to be paid in full at the end of each month. Strangely, revolving credit was never popular in Korea. Koreans in fact were using their cards mostly for cash advances, a very dangerous habit.

The government was pushing the use of credit cards. It wanted to change the cash-only payment patterns which were creating a huge black economy and were making tax evasion too easy.

From 2001, another reason for the government to support card growth was domestic consumption. The U. S. economy was retreating, and Korea was still very dependent on its exports to the United States. The only way to keep the traditional high growth that the Korean economy needed was to increase domestic consumption. The government thought that credit card utilization to support consumer spending would fuel the economy, especially in a country with a traditionally high savings rate and where most people had no credit usage. A tax rebate was even given to anybody using their credit card to buy goods instead of using cash.

Koreans began to use their credit cards for purchases, but just enough to get this tax rebate benefit, while using the cash advance feature indiscriminately. For many cardholders, it reached a level comparable to many months' salary, and obviously being unable to pay off balances at the end of each month, they were drawing on other cards to reimburse the first ones.

Pushed by strong competition, issuance of cards continued at the same rhythm until eventually delinquency caught up with the cardholders. Then, the reduction in credit lines by one issuer created a nonperforming loan with others. The snowball had started, and the growth spiral quickly became a vicious circle.

Korea First Bank was a very different credit card issuer. We had decided our growth in retail assets would primarily be in secured lending through residential mortgages (with barely more than a 1.5 percent margin and low risk) and not through credit card advances (with a 15 percent margin and significantly higher risks). The size of client assets growth we were targeting would have made any other strategy suicidal.

Some had been critical of our slower growth in this unsecured product while others were apparently growing fast in volumes and profits, but we were reluctant to develop our unsecured loan and credit card portfolio before creating rigorous risk management in this area. This slow start saved us.

It was a much smaller part of all our outstanding unsecured consumer assets. Combined unsecured assets represented only 15 percent of our total retail assets and credit card advances half of that. Keith Shachat kept his models updated and was applying them online with absolutely no local decision allowed to counter his models. All other banks and credit card companies were highly decentralized and were not using any in-house risk models. Consequently, our growth in this area was well below the market growth and less risky.

When the crisis unfolded, market delinquency ratios went through the roof to levels not seen even in the *tequila crisis* in Mexico. We were quite happy to have been much more prudent in issuing cards and more specifically in the credit limits for our individual clients and to have gotten ourselves out of the bulk refinancing of the non-bank consumer firms. The year before, we had had Won 5 trillion in bulk refinancing for credit cards companies, who were now in deep trouble.

But a national crisis spares no one, and even if our delinquency rates were much smaller than our competitors', they still increased to unacceptable levels. At the end of 2003, in spite of the increase in our loan volumes and margins, which had increased our operating margin by 73 percent, our profit before taxes (EBIT) was flat. Growth in our operating margin was completely absorbed by higher provisioning needed on unsecured retail loans and card advances outstanding.

Our risk models were very discriminating. They allowed us to know what segments of the population had lower delinquency. That was invaluable. Our information was continuously updated with new data, but these models could not forecast the total change in consumer behavior that took place.

Worse for everyone, the credit card companies were systematically postponing recognition of any delinquency problems. We knew what was happening, and we were continually tightening our underwriting criteria. But the magnitude of the crisis and the number of the actual delinquents was not possible to forecast.

But here also our approach was quite different from the other bank and credit card company issuers. We recognized delinquencies immediately, and over-reserved them (more than the regulatory requirement), while the other issuers, were not reserving , many of them were not able to do it without going to bankruptcy, or recognizing the delinquencies, and were re-aging these credits massively. Re-aging in this context meant that when a client was not able to pay the monthly bill, instead of declaring the delinquency, stopping the accrual of the interest, and putting aside a much higher reserve for possible loan loss, the issuers were automatically granting an extension of the amount due into a card-loan of one year, capitalizing the principal and interest due into this new loan. This new loan effectively refinanced the outstanding credit card debt. This process hid NPLs, and delinquency rates in truth exceeded 30 percent in most specialized issuers.

Not permitted in these circumstances in most countries, this process artificially increased the issuers' profitability by recognizing interest not paid as well as the omission of the required additional reserve while boosting balance sheets with larger but unrecoverable loans outstanding. This type of re-aging hid the actual status of the individual clients from the market, giving other lenders a false sense of security in continuing to grant other loans or credit cards to these borrowers.

Our policy of transparency forced us to over-reserve for the first few months. After increasing our reserves way above the required regulatory levels (12 percent for short-term delinquency up to ninety days and 50 percent for delinquents past due more than ninety days and less than one hundred eighty), to our own levels of 20 percent for past dues up to ninety days, and 90 percent for those over ninety days and less than one hundred eighty. With this scenario, we decided to immediately sell all credit card outstanding debt past due for more than ninety days, all that without any re-aging of the portfolio. With this harsh policy we were assured of a much faster recovery, and we still were profitable in 2003.

Eventually, the lack of actual cash payments from their clients directly pushed the credit card issuers from having excellent but wholly artificial results into a liquidity crisis. This would have led to multiple bankruptcies in any other country, but we will see how the government reacted to this crisis.

The effects on the economy were naturally harsh. Growth in credit card utilization had helped increase domestic consumption dramatically for two years, but now the crisis had a terrible effect. Nearly 25 percent of the population became de facto delinquents, and another 25 percent reduced their consumption to financially support relatives who had bad debts. This brutal stop in consumption by 50 percent of the population riddled the economy with problems. With sales reducing sharply, corporations and SMEs saw their own liquidity and credit worthiness rapidly decline.

Fortunately, KFB continued to focus on the most secure part of the loan market: residential mortgages and prime corporations.

S. Y. Yang, the executive in charge of the branch network, was still not happy with our market share in mortgages. He asked the executive committee to consider lending in a much larger scale through a wholesale mortgage (WM) program.

A full study was completed and presented to the executive committee by S. Y. Yang and his wholesale mortgage specialist, Hong-Tae Park. This was a business very specific to Korea. Koreans were quickly becoming much wealthier and were moving to new or big cities, especially the ones around Seoul. Increasingly, younger couples were breaking with tradition that kept many generations under the same roof and were willing to buy new apartments exclusively for themselves.

Construction in Korea was largely handled by large companies, especially the subsidiaries of the bigger *chaebols*. These companies applied the industrial approach to apartment buildings. They were building in one program small cities comprised of ten or more very large buildings representing between five thousand and fifteen thousand apartments either on new land or by fully destroying and rebuilding a smaller but older city.

The financing was also industrialized with a one size fits all concept. If it was a reconstruction project, financing was granted to individual owners in phases: relocation payments, progressive payments, and finally full payment and re-occupation. If it was a new city, financing was directly granted to the new buyers. We studied the risks in each step, from the perfection of the securities to the guarantees, and created new procedures. We then created a specialized department, the wholesale mortgage department, led by H. T. Park, to manage and coordinate this activity nationwide. Only after we had put all the controls in place did we start operating for business.

Despite our conservative risk approach and policies, the aggressiveness of our officers and our ability to manage large number of loans, quickly made it a huge success, and volumes originated through this channel were added to our classic retail mortgage production. Our employees were working seven –days –a week. They were spending their weekends at the building sites, contacting builders, sellers, and clients, and actually selling mortgage loans there.

By year-end 2003, KFB's market share in mortgages reached 9 percent, from less than 1 percent at the end of 2001, with negligible NPLs. In fact, when taking into account recoveries post foreclosure and delinquent interest collected, the net effect was no net losses at all in our mortgage portfolio.

Because we screened all borrowers through our home-built credit data warehouse (and were consequently able to tighten our risk criteria on line when needed), we were also able to continue lending throughout the credit card crisis, while our competitors, who still retained their decentralized organization, were obliged to choose to lend or not and very often were obliged to stop all new lending.

We had also centralized all collections at the CSCs. This activity involved collecting all payments, both interest and principal, on loans not received on the due dates. This allowed our branch managers to focus on selling instead of the growing burden of increasing collection activity. Our branch managers were thinking growth and opportunities, while the competitors were too busy collecting to actually compete.

With the continuing crisis, our competitors were attempting to find the responsible parties for these losses and often found the branch managers responsible. Without credit authority, our branch managers were only responsible for applying the rules, not making the decisions, and therefore could not be held responsible for the delinquencies.

At the same time, a new problem arose. This was a good problem though, in that our loan production was so strong that our capital ratios were declining. To remedy this without slowing our strong growth, we decided to issue a hybrid tier 1 international bond. This was a deeply subordinated bond that could for international bank ratios be considered as tier 1 capital, like equity. But even with this, it would be not enough if loan production kept its strong pace, and so we began to prepare for securitization of some of our mortgage assets in 2004.

With the credit card crisis, we spent a lot of time focusing on retail risks and opportunities, while the corporate side of the bank was also growing quite well. We had avoided all the large corporate failures, such as SK Global and LG Card, by sticking to our policies of no risk concentrations, our own in-house analysis of both group and subsidiary financial status, and refusal to be coerced in any way, by any party. Each year the Central Bank rated our new corporate NPLs by as much as twenty times smaller than our competitors' average new NPLs.

Even considering this, we were growing faster and in the more profitable part of the business: structured finance. There was less competition, better margins, and our loans were better secured. Nobody considered now that we were not involved in corporate lending. We were just doing it differently.

In keeping with our usual policies, we never entered a business until we were ready with internal controls and systems. After the completion of Kondor Plus, our traders were back to business. Our BOD approved some small limits for foreign exchange trading and government bond trading, and we established a small special bonus pool for the trading room, a revolution at KFB. The results were spectacular given the low level of risk taken. Our traders were making money; not large amounts, but much more than planned.

When Mr. Kim became the new chairman of the union, one of his first demands was to organize a huge employee festival by inviting all employees and their families to one location to reinforce solidarity and raise morale. This would be a demonstration of how management and the union had reconciled.

At first I thought it was a crazy idea, having more than fifteen thousand people in one place. But speaking with our human resources experts, I discovered that these huge meetings were done by other banks and industrial companies and were part of Korean tradition.

I studied it, thinking in a more open minded way, and I found a lot of positives in this idea. My priority had been employee morale, to forget the traumatism and the 1997 shame. I was in the middle of difficult discussions with the union and the employees about the progressive severance program, and this event would both improve relations and mutual understanding, and the cost budgeted for that day was nothing compared to the amounts involved in the progressive severance negotiation.

We decided to go ahead for KFB's seventy-fourth anniversary in July, congregating most employees at Everland (an amusement park comparable to Disneyland, close to Seoul), with the balance of the employees outside of the Seoul area in two similar locations in the south of the country. Employees, their spouses, and children were all invited to enjoy the park starting early in the morning, with everybody gathering around four PM in a huge area with seating for thirteen thousand. A scenic stage for speeches, games, and professional performers was also constructed, and a full audio/video link with the other parks allowing the people there to watch and participate, albeit from a distance.

The union chairman and I visited all three locations, shaking hands, congratulating employees, spouses, and children. Despite the large retinue following me everywhere (including HR people, interpreters, union staff, regional managers, etc.), it quickly became more personal for me with employees who were happy to introduce their family. All were smiling and repeating that they were once again proud to be part of *Cheil Eunheng* (the First Bank).

At four PM, in front of thirteen thousand people, with two thousand more attending via video link, I gave a speech underscoring how well they were doing and that they should be very proud of their hard work, that *Cheil Eunheng* was again becoming the First Bank (true to its identity), and that we were all one big family. The chairman of the union, Mr. Kim, spoke in the same tone, and it was what they had been expecting. The performances and shows were great, and all were happy to see me and the executives with their families sharing the same shows, reacting like Koreans. My wife, being in France for family reasons, was unfortunately not able to attend.

I was happy I had agreed to this festival. It boosted morale, and while the other banks were retreating, bruised by the credit card crisis, we were continuing to aggressively push ahead.

Toward the end of 2003, I finally decided to show the bank officers the numbers I was doing for myself and the board that compared our ratios with our competitors', especially the ratio I considered the most important leading indicator for KFB: the client-assets per employee ratio. For comparison purposes, I used only the number of full-time employees, the only thing the Korean banks published.

When I arrived, this ratio stood at Won 2.6 billion per employee, while the other banks' ratios were averaging Won 5.9 billion. By the end of 2003, we had reached Won 6.4 billion, while the others were now averaging Won 8 billion. The most important thing was that the difference was shrinking fast.

Despite this, our first employee poll, in 2003, showed continued trauma from the 1997 crisis, and the following terrible years; a complete picture with low self esteem, a lack of confidence, and multiple questions about the future.

Korea, the Country

First and above all, Korea was the country of miracle growth. Very few countries have shown this level of growth in the past forty years. GDP per capita was only $100 in 1963, and yet by 2004 it had reached $19,300, higher than the EU average GDP per capita.

Korea was also a country of many challenges. During the 1960s and 1970s they had one goal and only one: to develop the country. Every Korean was highly focused on it. It was either that or die of cold and malnutrition before forty.

Fortunately scholars were always respected, and education had always been a priority. Higher education and an enlightened dictatorship allowed the *chaebols* to grow, and to grow very fast, without any natural resources. Korea came from nowhere in term of industrialization to become one of the leading countries that manufactured clothing, chemical products, steel, ship-building, cars, electronics, and later, computer chips, flat screens, cell phones, and many more products with their own brands with which we are now very familiar.

In the 1980s Korea had a surprising number of very large companies. Due to the lack of equity, they were highly over-leveraged but dynamic and growing, thanks to the unlimited liquidity given to them by the banks and a cheap, efficient and educated labor force, two decisive competitive advantages.

Democracy and an improving standard of living increased labor costs, and the unions continued to push for more employee-friendly laws. By the end of the 1990s, the competitive advantage linked to lower labor costs had disappeared, at least for the larger companies, while the others (without unions) were still working as before. More and more of the larger companies reorganized as they needed to make good use of cheap subcontractors, even if the local industrial model was culturally based more on vertical integration.

Natural selection of the industrial groups began, accelerated by the 1997 crisis. The weakest disappeared, the ones that could be saved were saved by the government, and the strongest continued to expand. But the impact on the banking system was devastating, and the virtual bankruptcy of all the banks clearly demonstrated the limits of the industrial model. After reaching a certain level of development, *Korea, Inc.* could no longer continue as before. A new system closer to market principles and open to competition needed to be created in order to both attract capital and to export into developed countries, both vital needs for Korea, which always needed to import raw materials.

With practically no safety net, the Korean system worked only with high growth, and the engine of this growth was exports. When the dot-com bubble collapsed demand in the United States reduced, and the only short term solution for Korea was to push internal demand. Credit card expansion had to be understood in this context. Later, Korean companies redeployed their trading skills to take advantage of China's expansion, and between 2001 and 2005, China passed from being Korea's tenth most important client to being number one.

But with a workforce now nearly as costly as Europe's, Korean companies needed more and more capital, and FDI was difficult to attract without accepting some basic rules, one of which was sharing control.

Korea was now in the strange situation where half of its administration was desperately trying to attract foreign direct investments (FDI) and to project a modern image, while the other half was trying to maintain its power, making things work like before and refusing any foreign intrusion. This schizophrenia, both in the administration and in the media, was also a reflection of public opinion made worse by the generation gap.

Korea's development was not linear but rather subject to many cycles. Since 1997, we saw successively the fall of the *chaebols,* the comeback of the strongest *chaebols,* the bankruptcy of the banking system and its reconstruction stronger than ever, and a remarkable recovery from the boom of the exports to the United States and their subsequent stagnation, with the gap being filled by domestic demand first and then by exports to China.

Following the boom in domestic consumption, which was mainly financed by the excess in consumer spending, the credit card crisis virtually bankrupted 25 percent, and close to half the population drastically reduced its spending in 2003. The first victims were the SMEs, the self-employed, and the mom-and-pop stores. They were the least capitalized and the most fragile part of the economy with no export, no safety net, and no working capital to survive the storm.

The government could not stand by and watch this, so they first tried to encourage the banks to support the SMEs, just like before. They reduced interest rates in the hope of bringing down the debt burden. Most of the effect increased the demand for mortgages, so new anti-mortgage rules were created, thereby slowing the only part of the domestic economy that was growing well.

With its economy still fragile and the size of the country still relatively small, the Korean government was again obliged to interfere with the economy. But this time, it was a more complex economy as it was more linked to the outside world. Korea could no longer be centrally managed as it was in the 1970s.

Government intervention had to be more market–oriented, a difficult change for an administration used to giving direct orders. More often, market-like actions were too strong or followed with too many controls, so that they solved one problem only to create another one. This was the case in the credit card and mortgage markets.

In spite of its fragility and its cycles, the Korean economy had grown faster than most, recovering from the 1997 crisis faster than any other country. Thanks to the highly-educated nature of the workforce and the local work ethic, together with the dynamism and agility of Korean businessmen, they were able to take advantage of China's proximity and manage quite well the most difficult problems, such as the technology transfer of industrial production like textiles to China. Currently, many Korean companies maintain R&D and marketing while all production has been transferred.

Korea will likely face new challenges in the future, the most difficult ones being increases in energy costs, the continuing evolution of China, and the future of North Korea.

Increases in energy costs will penalize Korea as it relies on imported energy. But this is not unique to Korea, and I am convinced Korean enterprises will be able to compensate for these increases.

China is quite a different subject. Today, Koreans have the opportunity to produce low tech at low cost in China, but China, with its unlimited workforce and quick learning curve is already a formidable competitor, and the tech gap is shrinking. Having its largest client become its number 1 competitor will be a serious challenge for Korea ...

North Korea is also a dangerous neighbor, and not only on the military front. It has always been a subject that most Koreans avoid; even pronouncing the name was outlawed during the dictatorial years. Despite this, there are a lot of mixed feelings. The North Koreans have been altogether unpredictable foes, murderers, brothers, and poor brothers. Even with all of this, everyone in South Korea believes that one day Korea will be reunited.

The most pessimistic people imagine reunification happening very quickly. They calculate that it will take more than one generation to even get back at the current South Korean level of life after the economic fallout from reunification. Others believe that economic support to North-Korea today will help reduce the cost of future reunification by hoping that this transitory period of economic cooperation might last long enough to get North Korea to an economic level closer to the South.

Strangely, most consider North Korea more as an economic sword of Damocles than a military risk, despite experiencing few actual skirmishes every year which leave a few dead each time and the terrible open nuclear question.

Banks in Korea

At the end of the nineteenth century and in most of the twentieth, Korea was a very poor country, and the few banks created were mostly savings institutions. These were later converted into banks. Their role was to gather deposits from individuals while only providing them very basic services. Later, during the country's industrialization period, the government pushed the banks to use this liquidity to support the country's industrialization. It was the only possible way, as there was no accumulated wealth and thus no equity, no financial market, and virtually non-existent international relations.

Banks became identified with certain industrial groups and were lending almost without limit to these groups while participating in other groups' lending pools. Traditional conservative banking methodology of capping the maximum risk per borrower and risk spreading could not be applied even if the bank managers might have wanted it. There were too few companies in Korea, too few banks, and only a few industries that were actually developed, including textiles, construction and engineering, steel, cars, ships, electric appliances, and later electronics.

It was impossible to limit the risks to one industry to a percentage of each bank's capital. The banks had very limited capital, and were lending a multiple of it to each group. Even that was not enough for these new industrial colossi whose size quickly became disproportioned to the size of the country economy and its financial system.

As they were not managed using international standards, banks could not get large international financing without the explicit or implicit commitment of the government. Like in France after the Second World War, government-owned development banks (e.g., KDB) were created to use the explicit government guaranty in the global markets. Bank of Korea became the Central Bank, but also had the foreign exchange monopoly. This was a critical role in a country with strict exchange controls but with a willingness to develop exports in order to pay for the much-needed imports of food and raw materials.

The system worked until the 1997 crisis, when the banks found themselves with large commercial customers unable to even pay interest due on their loans. The recognition of these nonperforming loans was impossible. It would have meant reserving for these loans and bonds in amounts much larger than the banks could afford, a multiple of their capital, and it would have created losses much higher than the combined capital of all the banks, meaning the shutdown or collapse of the banking system and a full financial panic which would bring the risk at the size of the banks' total balance sheet. This was unthinkable.

The only solution was to create two government entities, the KDIC and Kamco, to buy bad debt, bonds, shares of problem enterprises, and to try to keep the system operating without recognizing any large bankruptcy while accepting a temporary huge under-reserving by the banks.

Korea needed foreign currency to continue its raw material imports, and so it borrowed from the International Monetary Fund (IMF). The IMF must have recognized that this policy was the only possible one given the circumstances, but to reestablish Korea's image and to try to extricate themselves from these hidden bankruptcies, the IMF demanded a swift clean-up of the banking system. This classic requirement meant a recapitalization of the banks, the introduction of risk management standards, an increase in reserving to the appropriate levels, and the privatization and accountability of the banks with an end to all government non-market-oriented intervention on the banks.

The Korean government was aware of the urgency of the situation. Their international ratings had dropped dramatically, and it was difficult even for the government to raise money in the international markets.

A few smaller banks were merged to create a larger state-owned bank, renamed Woori Bank (that could be translated to "our bank"). Two large banks, Kookmin and H&CB (the bank that had the monopoly on individual mortgages) were merged in the new Kookmin Bank. Hana Bank was encouraged to buy a few smaller banks. But the largest problems still existed. Those were ChoHeung Bank, Korea

First Bank, Seoul Bank, and Korea Exchange Bank (KEB was the spin off of the Bank of Korea foreign exchange monopoly that became a full corporate bank).

Many contacts by the government with international banks were unfruitful. It was not an easy proposition for large public banks to understand the risks of these troubled banks, as it was virtually impossible to measure from the outside the extent of the problems and thus to reasonably evaluate the time needed for a turnaround. That proposition could not be attractive for large publicly traded banks. There was too much imprecision for the stock market.

Korea, counter to its culture, then made a very courageous decision. They organized an auction process for their biggest problem institution, the Korea First Bank. In spite of bad press and alienated domestic public opinion, the auction proceeded until the eventual sale of 50.1 percent of KFB to Newbridge Capital Asia, a U.S.-based private equity fund linked to the Texas Pacific Group, later to become known as TPG.

The government granted a put option as part of the sale, and in retaining 49.9 percent of KFB (and its potential upside), it had to give Newbridge 100 percent voting rights and operating control. This sale played a major role in the quick reestablishment of Korea's international status and sovereign ratings.

But KFB quickly became for many a symbol of the unacceptable meddling by foreigners in the management of Korean "jewels." The government defended its position by assuring that this sale would bring international best practices and new financial techniques not only to KFB but to the whole banking system. The other side wanted nothing more than to prove that there were no new financial techniques and that foreigners could never do better than Koreans. This conviction, built up by isolationism and nationalism, was shared by so many people in the public and in the civil servant world that it was impossible for politicians and the news media to attack it directly.

The credit card crisis demonstrated once again the urgent need for quickly finishing the restructuring of the banking industry. After many unfruitful attempts to sell Seoul Bank to international investors, it was eventually sold to the Hana Bank, with government help. ChoHeung Bank was sold to another Korean bank, the Shinhan Bank. The remaining bank, the Korea Exchange Bank (KEB), was put up for sale, and a majority position was sold to Lone Star, another U.S.-based private equity fund. The precedent of KFB and the beginning of the credit card crisis without a doubt facilitated the KEB sale process. But KEB had once been part of Bank of Korea and had the monopoly of foreign exchange. These strategic and national images are difficult to erase in Korea and made in my mind its further sale to a foreign international bank difficult to imagine.

Following these sales the banking industry began to look more stable, with four large banks (Kookmin, Shinhan-ChoHeung, Woori, and Hana-Seoul) and three foreign-controlled banks (Korea First and Korea Exchange controlled by private equity groups and Koram, previously Bank of America Korea, which was later sold to Citigroup). Not counted in this picture were the two large cooperative banks (agricultural and fisheries) and a few much smaller regional banks.

It is interesting to note that even the four large Korean banks had a large majority of their shares owned by foreigners, but there was no connection in most Korean minds between the investor in stocks and the control and management of companies. This was even more true when speaking of banks, the image of the national public service.

To understand that paradox one has to remember the absence of accumulated wealth in Korea and the construction of the *chaebols* on very limited equity brought by the founding families. Then these fast growing groups had to look for debt, and more debt, and later equity, but that was thought of more as a financing tool than part of the ownership, which would mean an unthinkable power sharing.

This conception was beginning to recess in few economic circles. I experienced that in some of my lectures but not yet by far in the general public or even in the universities where some students' reactions to my lectures hinted that some assimilated the power sharing in Korean companies to a foreign plot to spoil Korea. Recently, courts began to criticize the staggering disproportion of ownership and management power the founding families have in the *chaebols*, but that mostly targeted tax evasion and the protection of Korean minority shareholders is just beginning to be considered. The protection of the foreign shareholders is still far away, a generation away I suppose, the time for general public opinion to go from nationalism to globalization.

This situation is reflected in the stock market value. Korean companies, even extraordinarily performing ones, trade at a lower multiple than companies in developed countries. This is widely called the Korean discount.

After these mergers and acquisitions, banks were better able to reduce costs and progressively increase reserves while investing in technology and modernizing their structures. But the economic cycles are short in Korea, and a succession of big NPLs (e.g., SK Global, LG Card) and the credit card crisis continued to shake the system. Fortunately, it was a much stronger system compared to 1997.

The credit card crisis was a tough period, with 25 percent of the population virtually in personal bankruptcy and all credit card companies technically bankrupt, including Samsung Card, LG Card, Kookmin Card, and KEB Card, to look only at the largest specialized companies.

Once again, it was impossible for these companies to immediately recognize the NPLs and the resulting losses; they would have been out of business. The banks with large loans outstanding to credit card clients and to credit card companies would have been obliged to reserve their outstanding balances and would have difficulties surviving themselves. KFB was in an enviable but unique position in that it had stopped lending bulk loans to credit card companies, and it was immediately able to recognize and fully reserve for its share of the problems of credit card clients above the statutory guideline levels.

The government came to the rescue again, succeeding even if not by way of transparency and market-oriented action. Contradictory regulations, officially asking for higher reserves while accepting de facto re-aging of NPLs, permitted the credit card companies to stay alive while corporate solutions were found. Banks were pushed to absorb their card subsidiaries even if they did not hold a majority position. Samsung Card was left aside, Samsung was rich enough to pay for its subsidiary needs even if it was not at all appreciated by other members in their group. The last one, and the one in the worst shape, was LG Card.

A full support from the LG Group would not have been enough and would jeopardize this bright industrial conglomerate. Shareholders and banks were invited to swap debt for equity and eventually to subscribe for new equity. The future of LG Card was still not easy to predict. Fortunately, KFB was no longer a creditor of LG Card and so was not part of the debt-for-equity swaps or any later restructuring, but we stayed one of their main banks for operating purposes.

ALM, a Capital Subject for a Bank

Assets and Liabilities Management (ALM) and gapping are very technical subjects, but because of their importance for Korea First Bank, I think they need some explanation here. Having previously been treasurer of a large international bank, I had many occasions to work on these subjects. This had been quite useful and had not been the case for my predecessor.

ALM is the action of managing risks generated by the different profiles of the assets and the liabilities of a bank.

The assets are the outstanding loans granted and bonds bought and more generally all claims that the bank owns and should receive back one day. They have specific maturities, and their rates might be fixed or floating (which means revised generally every three months by applying a pre-defined market reference—labor, for example). In the same way, a bank's liabilities are the bonds issued by the bank, certificates of deposit, time deposits, and all the debts the bank will have to re-pay. They have their own maturities with fixed or floating rates.

But some liabilities, including savings accounts and checking accounts, usually do not have any contractual maturity. They can be withdrawn at any time, but their large number and historic behavior allow a statistical approach, and interest rates paid are low and follow market changes only softly.

A bank that has only one-time deposit with a rate fixed for one year and that invests this money in government bills for one month at the monthly market rate would have some risk. Not credit risk—the government bill is not a risk, at least in local currency; not liquidity risk as long as the money is reimbursed every month and re-invested until the time deposit matures; but a large interest risk: if market rates decline, revenues from the bills would decline every month, while the time deposit would cost the same price and potentially create a loss.

Also, in most cases, long-term rates are higher than short-term rates. A bank would incur an extra cost by a structural negative difference (called the yield curve differential) between the cost of one-year money and the revenue based on one-month money (in this case, it would be what is called the short-term risk-free rate). This structural cost and the larger interest risk can be seen as the cost of the bank's extra liquidity, the ability to have every month the money back and be free to use it until the further maturity of the deposit.

This simple example is easy to grasp, but a large bank has thousands of loans and deposits with different characteristics maturing every day.

To analyze these risks the first task is to be able to track them all and have a detailed differentiated schedule of all assets and all liabilities in two ways: by final maturity to track the liquidity vulnerability, and by rate change to track the rate vulnerability. So a three-year loan with a rate adjusted every three months would be on the three-year line in the liquidity schedule and on the three-month line in the rate schedule.

The off-balance sheet commitments have to be included in these schedules with their probability of usage...

Both schedules need a specific study for the savings and checking accounts which do not have any contractual maturity or contractual rate. The stability of the outstanding and the fidelity of clients have to be studied, and some statistical analysis will help the decision on how to consider these important amounts and at what maturity the bank should assimilate them.

For KFB the client base was very stable, with clients who stayed through the crisis and the period following immediately. When the bank was not investing and was plagued by very low staff morale, they showed their unshakable fidelity. They were not going to leave the bank (or at least not any faster than the regular turnover). We decided, conservatively, that the stable part of these accounts should be considered as five-year money for liquidity purposes. For the internal rate schedule, we defined a progressive evolution based on the maturity decided.

The gap is the list of the monthly/yearly balances for each schedule. The bank could be "long" Won 5 trillion in the first year (more assets maturing than liabilities), and "short" Won 3 trillion the second year (more liabilities maturing than assets). In each schedule these balances would show the rate vulnerability of the bank as well as the liquidity vulnerability.

ALM is thus the management of these gaps in order to reduce vulnerabilities and to make money from it wherever possible.

In KFB's case, in 2002, when we were able to look precisely at the gaps, the bank showed huge liquidity. Half of the total liabilities (an amount close to Won 12 trillion) had very long maturities of at least five years, while the assets had much shorter maturities. Won 5 trillion of KDIC bonds were to be reimbursed within one year, and the bulk loan and corporate loan portfolios were for mostly short-term advances within one year. This situation introduced terrible vulnerability in terms of rates, with three month's interest received instead of long-term stable rates.

Another way to see this situation, for the non-specialist, is to consider checking and saving balances as low-rate deposits but with a large network fixed cost. When market rates go down costs are not changed much, but the revenues on the loans (funded with this money) decline, and operating profit declines with them.

191

So our conclusion was that KFB was excessively vulnerable at any decrease in market interest rates. That, unfortunately, confirmed my early thoughts and was why at the BOD meetings I always asked management to buy government securities when the rates were high.

The size of this mismatch made hedging practically impossible, especially in a small capital market like the local Korean Won market. My first action as CEO was to buy about Won 2 trillion in government securities with fixed three- and five-year rates while asking the BOD to increase our limits to allow us to buy more. Unfortunately, this kind of large investment takes time. During this whole period market rates were declining, so we continued to buy more but at lower rates. When the KDIC bonds were fully repaid in December 2002 we had to buy more government securities, but the market rates had dramatically decreased, and the level of remuneration we got was quite low.

The other action possible was to offer to clients fixed-rate loans for two to five years. We offered them to corporate clients but succeeded only in the structured financing area, which made these products even more important for us. We offered fixed rates to retail clients as well. It was normal for unsecured loans, but the amounts were so small that they would not have any noticeable impact on the bank's ALM. We then proposed fixed-rate features for the early periods in our mortgages.

In Korea, strangely, mortgage contracts had always been done with rates adjusted every three months, with maturities limited to only three years, usually in bullet loan format (loans with only one repayment at maturity). We proposed amortizing loans for all maturities up to thirty years and a fixed rate for the first one to five years. Unfortunately, habit was so strong that it took us a long time to convince clients that they were better of with a long-term mortgage which could be reimbursed at any time than with a short-term mortgage that might push them out of their homes if banks refused to refinance at the end of the three-year maturity.

It was the same thing with the rates. Consumers had such a short-term view that they preferred a variable rate which seemed lower at the beginning than a fixed rate, an attitude which can be very costly in increasing rate environment, as the sub-prime crisis in the United States has showed. Still, we succeeded in selling a few hybrid (variable-rate mortgages with a fixed-rate period at the beginning), and that helped reduce our gap.

We naturally looked for other hedges, but it was not an easy task when taking into account the size of the local Won market and generally accepted Korean accounting principles (GAAP). In fact, the only easy action was to swap all long-term liabilities issued (bonds, financial debentures, and long-term time deposits of a certain size) to variable rates as soon as we could. Even after these hedges, our position was still highly vulnerable to rate decreases.

We evaluated the cost of this vulnerability at Won 1 billion a month for every ten cent decrease in the three-month CD market rate (the usual reference rate in Korea). Market rates went down by about 2 percent between the beginning of 2002 and the end of 2004, creating a vicious spiral that negatively impacted a large part of the volume and efficiency gains that Korea First Bank made during that period.

The positive side of this situation was that the variable rates worked automatically in favor of the bank when market rates went up, and we could hope for that as they were currently by far at the lowest market rate level ever reached in Korea. In fact, we actually saw this virtuous spiral beginning to work in the first quarter of 2005, just after the sale to Standard Chartered Bank.

Korea First Bank Seventy-Fifth Anniversary Ceremony

Annie Cohen and Elizabeth Barker in the Traditional
Hanbok

Robert Cohen in the Traditional Korean Costume

Chapter 6

2004, Korea First Bank is First

In 2004, the bank continued its growth in the retail business, primarily in residential mortgages --This was deliberate, as we wanted to avoid the last convulsions of the credit card crisis -- and in corporate finance, with an even higher proportion of structured financing transactions. It became obvious that we were going to exceed the original "too optimistic" volume goal for 2004, and the astonished employees were happy and began to believe that I was a kind of magician.

The second employee opinion poll done in the first half of 2004 showed a dramatic shift. Confidence was returning, and the employees were losing their feeling of inferiority, something that had overwhelmed them since the 1997 crisis. KFB's remarkable quarterly results, when compared with the other Korean banks, were finally sinking in.

The bank's public image was also beginning to improve. The general public was beginning to lose the *Tears* image, replacing it with a more modern, aggressive, and successful image of the bank, finally!

Together with McCann's, our advertisement agency, we had been working on our image from the beginning, but the general public view of the bank was so tarnished by the crisis that for a long time we had felt that we would never be able to change this perception. Fortunately, our patience and confidence in what we were doing was paying off.

At the end of 2002 we had decided on a publicity strategy featuring the former captain of the Korean soccer team, who had shocked the world by reaching the semi-finals of the 2002 World Cup. Hong Myong-Bo was the most respected athlete in Korea, as well as being a very strong advocate for under-privileged children. Our TV and print ads worked extremely well, and we continued this strategy into 2003 and beyond, capitalizing on our new strong reputation in residential mortgage as well as the professional and dynamic nature of our employees.

We decided to use 2004, our seventy-fifth anniversary, to leverage our profile further by publicizing to all just how many accomplishments the bank had achieved. Our target was always intended to be both internal as well as external, and we succeeded.

The following was how we portrayed these accomplishments.
(presented here in two pages)

There is a reaso

Financial Transparency & Corporate Governance

▶ Best capitalized bank in Korea (BIS)

▶ First in Korea with non-executive board of directors

▶ Best-priced Asian issuance of Hybrid Tier 1 bonds (10 X oversubscribed)

▶ Most advanced financial reporting
- Monthly financial statements in 3 days
- Product & account profitability analysis
- Activity-based costing
- Consolidated business planning
- Sophisticated budgeting system

Risk Management

▶ Lowest non-performing loan ratio in Korea

▶ Best loan provision coverage in Korea

▶ Lowest credit card delinquency in Korea

▶ First structured risk-based pricing in Korea

▶ First online credit decisions in Korea

▶ Centralized & online underwriting systems

제일은행
KOREA FIRST BANK

n why FIRST is in our name!

Organization & Process

▶ First integrated centralized service centers in Korea

▶ 2004 "Q-Service" (World Best) award Class Certification AAA : For Call Center (KMA)

▶ 2004 Customer Satisfaction Management Award Segmented Award : Customer Value Added (CVA) Grand Prize (KMA)

▶ First to automate loan process & underwriting

▶ Most advanced loan collections system & strategy

▶ First to utilize target marketing with CRM data mining tools

▶ First to implement PIN customer security system

▶ 2004 Social Contribution Corporate Award Segmentted Award: Social-welfare Grand Prize (Hankyung)

Products & Services

▶ Y2004 Hit Product "Double Plus Passbook" -Maekyung Economic Daily, KyungHyang Newspaper

▶ First bank to launch long-term installment mortgage loans in Korea : "First Home Loan" (FHL)

▶ First bank to issue offshore MBS

▶ First bank to launch VISA "Check Card with IC Chips"

▶ First to offer interest rebates to borrowers with good payment records & deposit balances : "Cash-back FCL"

▶ First to offer interest rebates for mortgage borrowers as a benefit for card usage : "Mortgage Saver"

▶ 2000 Hankook Newspaper "Web Award" for best E-banking website

▶ First to launch automated service "Giro CD" for utility, tax & other payments

▶ ISO 9001 Certification consulting & loan processing services (BSI Korea)

Information Technology

▶ New point-of-sale workstations throughout branch network

▶ First bank to adapt middleware solution for legacy system

▶ First bank to achieve CMMI Level 3 certifications

▶ First bank to launch Business Continuity Planning project

▶ First bank to successfully rollout data warehouse & data mining tools

▶ 2004 CRM Award Financial Grand Prize (The Federation of Korea Information Industries)

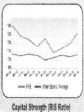

Capital Strength (BIS Ratio)

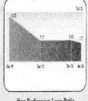

Non Performing Loan Ratio

Loan Growth

201

This poster was framed and hung in every one of our over four hundred offices, naturally in Korean, and was used as a print advertisement in newspapers, with a very large version covering one wall of the Lotte Hotel ballroom for our seventy-fifth anniversary reception.

From corporate governance to risk management, from financial disciplines to organization, from product range to technology applications, we were delivering the best international techniques in the Korean market that no other Korean bank had adopted by then.

Most importantly, this was supporting the rationale that the government gave for its decision to sell KFB to foreign investors. The government told the general public that KFB's investors would deliver new techniques while all the nationalist opponents were trying to show they would bring nothing new. These affirmations became for these reasons quite important from a political viewpoint and were in consequence powerful in lifting employee morale and customer confidence.

These two facts are the two most important factors for a bank's success. First, a bank is a service company, and without high employee morale there is no marketing action possible, especially in a sector where products proposed are essentially the same or at least very similar. Second, a bank needs deposits, and how did they attract new or large deposits without client confidence?

For the last time, I allowed myself to be convinced by the union chairman to hold another employee festival to celebrate the seventy-fifth anniversary of the bank, this time having all employees and their families at Everland, Korea's equivalent of Disneyland. Fifteen thousand people!

This celebration was even more spectacular than the previous one. Morale was up and going higher.

We also held a large reception at the Lotte Hotel for all our clients as well as local officials. It was difficult for many Koreans to admit that foreigners succeeded in turning around KFB, but most were beginning to admit privately that this was the case. Our risk management and our processes were given as examples. Newspapers no longer spoke about KFB as the troubled bank purchased by a foreign hedge fund, but rather as a very active bank with conservative risk management, which after the credit card crisis became less of a criticism.

At the reception mentioned earlier, our guest of honor was the governor of the central bank, Bank of Korea. Mr. Park Seung made a remarkable speech, going against all the preconceived ideas and images of KFB, and qualified us as one of the leading banks in terms and substance in asset quality, and complimented us for our advanced financial systems and international standards. He finished by saying that the video of *Tears* was becoming the video of glory, a strong booster effect on the morale of our employees!

Taking advantage of this change in public perception, we opened our private banking operations. It had taken us more than a year to find a qualified manager and prepare the needed structure. We wanted the manager to be a Korean, but no Korean (at least in Korea) actually had any experience in the wealth management area, as it was a new thing in Korea.

We needed to search among the Korean community externally, and we eventually found an experienced investment advisor/private banker ready to return to Korea with his family. We then needed to invest in the right software as well as hire or promote from within the future private bankers. Then we needed to train them. To kick off our strategy, we created two private banking centers in Seoul with ten specialists in each center.

We opened the centers in 2004, after two years of preparation work. Our image had changed for the better in the interim period. The professionalism of this approach paid off, and it was immediately a success.

In term of volumes, KFB had exceeded all my hopes, and we grew in spite of all the difficult economic cycles which affected Korea and the banking system. Both retail and corporate lending exceeded our plan, the one that many had considered as too aggressive and some even unreachable.

Our corporate client loan assets reached Won 11.6 trillion versus Won 10 trillion in the original plan, and our retail client assets reached Won 21 trillion versus the Won 18 trillion targeted. We were rolling..

We were simultaneously able to reduce the line called others, which included mostly non-interest-bearing assets: physical assets, real estate owned, and above all, outstanding in float in correspondent banks.

Actual Assets (in Trillion Won) at the End of Each Year

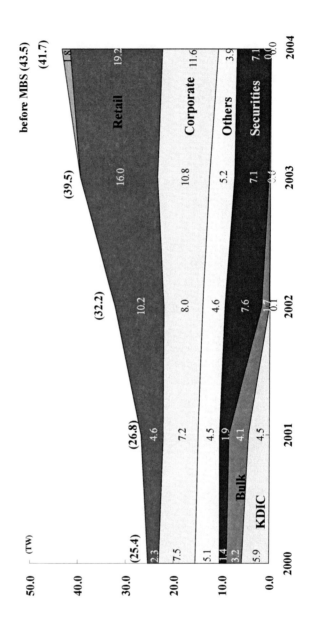

To be compared to my original "too optimistic" plan which was:

1/1/2002	original Plan					
Trillions Wons	**2000**	**f 2001**	**P2002**	**P2003**	**P2004**	**P2005**
Large corporate	3.5	3	3.2	4	4.6	5
S M E	2.8	3.3	3.8	4.7	5.4	6
Retail	2.4	4.5	9.8	14	18	22
Sub Total client-assets	**8.7**	**10.8**	**16.8**	**22.7**	**28**	**33**
%		*0.24*	*0.56*	*0.35*	*0.23*	*0.18*
KDIC bonds	5.9	4.5	0	0	0	0
Bulk loans	3.2	4.1	2.3	1.3	0	0
other assets	6.4	5.5	5.7	5.5	5.5	5.5
Total assets	**24.2**	**24.9**	**24.8**	**29.5**	**33.5**	**38.5**
%		*0.03*	*0*	*0.19*	*0.14*	*0.15*
Total assets targeted	24.2	24.9	32	38	42	44.3
%		*0.03*	*0.29*	*0.19*	*0.11*	*0.05*
To inv est for li quidity			7.2	8.5	8.5	5.8

In 2004, we securitized Won 1.8 trillion of residential mortgages. We executed a full securitization: we sold the assets to a special purpose vehicle which then issued bonds representing the most senior trenches (which received AAA and AA ratings from the major international rating companies), and we then sold them to international investors but we bought back the subordinated debt: We still had no losses in our mortgage portfolio (after foreclosures), and we knew first-hand that the subordinated debt was an excellent risk with a great margin.

The securitization process in fact increased our profitability, because we could continue to actively originate loan assets without over-leveraging our balance sheet, providing us with affordable long-term AAA funding.

Giving the bank very positive exposure in the international financial markets, KFB's mortgage securitization was a success and reopened the Korean market to international investors. It was a first in all Asia.

By the end of 2004, KFB's share in the local residential mortgage market was exceeding 11 percent.

This tremendous growth was achieved without any staff increase and that naturally improved one of our key ratios: client assets per employee. This ratio was standing at less than 50 percent of our competitors' average in 2001, but by 2004 we had succeeded in achieving a ratio higher than four other Korean banks, and we were surpassed by only three banks, which had been more oriented than us toward large credits to large companies.

We tripled our client-assets-per-employee ratio, while no other bank got close to doubling this ratio during this period.

I was always amazed at how all our branch managers and officers followed this race and how focused they were on it not only at the bank level but also at the level of each unit.

In the head office, we no longer had to think in terms of staff reduction in the branches, but more of reallocation of staff to those units that were showing the higher growth.

The impregnation of our branch managers by these basic ratios and the importance given to them by the bank's management was enough to change dramatically their comportment. Branch managers no longer asked for more staff for comfort or to increase their relative position but only when really it was needed, when they knew the new revenues would pay for it.

Loans to Clients per Full-Time Employee

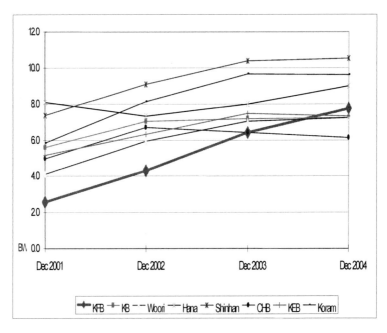

	KFB	KB	Woori	Hana	Shinhan	CHB	KEB	Citi Kor
Dec 2001	26	56	41	81	74	50	52	58
Dec 2002	43	70	59	73	91	67	63	81
Dec 2003	64	72	70	80	104	64	75	96
Dec 2004	78	72	72	90	105	61	73	NA

KFB: without Bulk & befor MBS, All: excluded call loan & RP

The excellent results shown above finally allowed us to go out and hire. We needed to correct our age pyramid and bring in talented younger officers to build a better structure for the next generation. We had hired one hundred new college graduates at the end of 2003 to show our confidence, and we authorized the hiring of two hundred at the end of 2004 to be sure that the market understood we were back, and that we would be hiring more talented people to protect our future. In a country where a very large majority of college graduates remained with their first employer, it was critical for us to fill the human gaps left by the crisis and the subsequent dark period.

The processes of hiring new employees and integrating these promotions were quite interesting, especially as I had required (against tradition) that at least one-third of the intake be women. HR and a few executives went on campus to attract students, just like in the United States, but that was where the analogy stopped.

The first group of one hundred newly hired graduates arrived in the bank at the end of December 2003. They were first sent (both men and women), on a full one-week commando-like training exercise with the army, close to the DMZ (armistice border with North Korea).

While I had been briefed about this custom, I was choked by the harsh images of this mid-winter training, in spite of my own military training. I decided to joke about it in order to understand their feelings, thinking about forbidding it for trainees the next year.

So, at my first presentation-training session with this group, I told them that I supposed they were happy with the vacation camp the bank had offered them even before they had begun to work. I got their story directly: walking in freezing water, hiding in the snow, walking in the mountains at all times, but mostly around three AM. But when I asked them if we should stop the tradition, their answer was unequivocally no. They felt that this tough week created, more than anything, a group cohesiveness, a team spirit, while promoting more equality between men (who had mandatory military service) and women. Even the people who suffered the most from this training defended it, so I decided to continue with the tradition for the next year. That time we hired two hundred young graduates.

The 2004 negotiation with the union was quite tense, first because for the first time since I had joined the bank we actually had to negotiate salary increases, as the agreement signed by my predecessor had expired; and second, I wanted to officially agree with the union on a demotion process. We were removing poorly performing branch managers and department heads, but we did not have any other acceptable position to give them and no legal way to push them to take casual retirement.

The chairman of the union had difficulty with these subjects. On the one hand, he understood very well our strange demography and that it was impossible to promote new managers without removing some (and the employees were requiring more promotions). On the other hand, it was difficult for a union to give more power to fire to the CEO.

Finally he took a courageous position, and we agreed to create a formal process to gradually reduce the salary of the poorest performers, using this, in fact, as a weapon to coerce them into choosing casual retirement immediately. The more months these officers stayed with the bank after this formal process of reducing their salary began, the more their retirement package and pension payout would have been reduced. Showing typical stoicism, the employees supported this agreement.

Our NPL ratio was the lowest amongst the banking industry in Korea, and after a limited spike during the credit card crisis we were just above 1 percent. This was two to three times less than the national average, even without counting in this average the non-bank credit card companies' NPLs.

But if we were well above plan in terms of volume and human productivity, we were still dragging in term of profitability. There were three reasons for this. The most important by far was the continuous fall in market interest rates. The three-year government bond was paying 3.28 percent at the end of 2004, less than what we were paying a ninety-day time deposit.

Our large government bond portfolio, which was needed for immediate liquidity, was bringing a negative margin, and our *gap* cost us Won 110 billion in 2004. This was Won 75 billion worse than in 2003. Our return on equity in 2004 stood slightly higher than 11 percent, but without this extraordinary market rate situation, our ROE would have been around 20 percent, much closer to our goal.

The other unplanned negative factors were mostly linked to Korean accounting and reserves required by the regulators for mortgages. Most of the loan originating costs had to be taken upfront, as well as the reserves. In order to generate large profits, one would have to stop new loan origination. But that would reduce long term profitability and would be bad for the future of the bank, and that was not our goal.

To make matters worse, the government increased the level of reserves for mortgages totally out of proportion with the risk taken in order to discourage financing for individual mortgages.

In most cases, it is the evaluation of the final risk taken which defines the need for reserves. In the case of residential mortgages in Korea, it would have been close to zero, especially when the law prevented financing higher than 60 percent of the price of any property and even a 40 percent loan-to-value restriction in some locations that were considered speculative. The new Basel II International Banking Rules were going in the opposite direction, by planning to reduce drastically the capital weighting and the reserves linked to individual conforming mortgages.

But I knew that these specific reductions of our apparent profitability were not so dramatic. The excess of provisions were creating de facto reserves and were staying in the bank. More, I knew that an international buyer focused on international rules would mentally reincorporate them in the bank value, sure to be able to make them reappear as a profit at the consolidated level.

The Sale

By 2004, both the management team and the board of directors were convinced that the rebuilding of the bank was done.

The infrastructure was now totally modernized: We had a highly functional and efficient centralized processing environment supported by a state-of-the-art IT and communication system as well as one of the best electronic banking capabilities in the market. We implemented an international standard continuity process to best survive any possible disaster, and we had a centralized but very responsive risk management process for both retail and corporate banking.

We could be proud of a modernized branch network totally focused on sales and client service with the largest range of products in Korea both in retail and specialized financing for corporations.

I could still see a few areas where we could improve. The SME were partly sacrificed by the Pro-Branch project that protected us when this market showed very high delinquency, but now we were only beginning our comeback to this important segment of clients. The trading activities had to be widened and deepened to allow us to capitalize fully on our new structure finance image and be a player in the growing Korean capital market, but both the recent situation of the bank and our BOD's natural inclination against concentrated and investment-banking-like risks, were preventing us from moving meaningfully in this direction, leaving that to the next owner. Finally, our new foray in wealth management was highly successful and could grow much more in a country were wealth was created fast.

The client-assets-per-employee ratio was going to be the best in Korea, especially when taking into account our very low risk   concentration and that exhibited our success in rebuilding the bank's balance sheet.

Our risks levels were so low (perhaps too low) that they were not even comparable to the other banks in Korea. In retail, we had at least Won 120 billion in excess reserves (thanks to the local regulation), and our corporate portfolio continually reflected a very low risk level and by far the lowest NPL ratio. We were reserving for all of it according to the highest of our two references: the best international practices and the Korean regulation. Finally, we still had practically no market risk on our books and no derivatives trading at all.

But these very low risk levels, this over reserving, and the low market rates were dampening our profitability, keeping it at a relatively low 11 percent ROE.

Both the executive team and I were convinced that this profile would be highly valuable for an international bank seeking to enter Korea in a major way with relatively low and well-identified risk levels. A strategic buyer would look at all these factors and recognize the potential to build a highly profitable bank off this solid base. I strongly defended this point of view at a strategy session with our key investors in the early fall of 2004.

Few days after, coincidentally, a large international bank approached our principal shareholder directly and some discussions began. These were informal at first, then more precise. During this period I had some meetings with top executives of the potential buyer, and my presentations provoked the enthusiasm I expected.

After a first period of exclusivity, this bank decided to begin the due diligence process but without any commitment given from either part.

Just after that, through an investment bank, another international bank approached our principal shareholder, and after few high level meetings joined the due diligence process.

It was naturally a difficult period, as I had to keep both management and the bank focused on business growth to ensure we could deliver what we regarded as a valuable asset. Nobody could predict whether a sale would happen, and so business as usual was critical. Interaction with the possible buyers was naturally burdensome as they always needed more information, and we needed to keep our employees' moral high and their minds focused.

The last point was obviously the most delicate and, for me, perhaps the most important. I vividly remembered from three years earlier how de-moralization and de-motivation of a sales force could spell disaster, so I increased communications, and while not being authorized to speak about possible acquirers, I began to speak about the future.

It was a question often asked, and I usually answered it by bringing the discussion back to the 2004 goal: When we reach our goal we will be a good bank, quite an attractive one.

From mid-2004, our volume goal was going to be met. I also knew that the branch managers were not responsible for the fall in market rates that were preventing us from reaching our profitability goal, so I began to speak about the next possible steps on our path too success back from the brink.

Everyone was aware that our principal investors would not keep their participation in the bank forever. Private equity funds have to return the funds to the investors and the government also wanted to be repaid, so it was only a question of when and how.

In one of our regular manager meetings, in front of six hundred officers, I began to talk candidly about the many possibilities in the future, whether it be acquisition by a Korean bank, a public listing (IPO) through the stock exchange, or the acquisition by an international bank seeking to increase its presence in the Korean market.

Our officers knew very well that a Korean bank would have to tackle all the redundancies of a merger, and that would mean a repetition of the ERPs and the likely disappearance of the bank as an entity. This was for all of them their worst fear, and I used that by repeating what I actually believed, that to reach our 2004 goal would help protect us against this eventuality by making KFB too expensive for a local bank acquirer, but also making our profile very attractive to an international bank.

In the second half of 2004, after eliminating the possibility of an acquisition by a Korean bank, I mostly presented the alternative between an independent life with our stock quoted on the stock exchange, with its glory but also its risks of possibly being bought later by a Korean bank, and on the other hand, the possibility of being bought by a big international bank, a strategic investor. That would bring a more complex matrix management system, but an international bank would have no redundancy in the local branch network in Korea. It would bring more international techniques to add to those already implemented and the capital for growth and continuity for the new KFB.

I did not hide from them the complexity of matrix management, explaining what it was and how different it was from the Korean hierarchy system. It was so distant from their culture that I was not sure if they fully understood it.

I answered questions as honestly as possible, and I went through the same exercise through questions asked at each officer and staff meeting going forward, including my meetings with the union and the young managers.

So when discussions with the potential buyers became more formal and public and when due diligence started, I spoke openly and more often about the process, and was happy to see that there had been no noticeable disturbance. The bank was still growing fast, and even those employees worried about the future and the uncertainties it would bring, were continuing to work with the same dedication.

We set up two separate off-site due diligence rooms, and the two banks look at our documents in an orderly way. We were proud to see that due diligence did not highlight any problems that might impact the acquisition value. Rather, the opposite occurred, and the price increased after the due diligence process.

I continually maintained the information flow with the executives, the officers, the union, and the employees all getting any public information fast and directly from me. Finally, one of the two banks participating in the due diligence process made a higher offer and it was accepted, by our board. The successful bidder was the Standard Chartered Bank.

The shareholders were due to receive close to four times the amount invested on January 1, 2000. The new valuation at about two times our net book value clearly demonstrated the buyers' high opinion in our rebuilding of the bank and importantly its future.. During the same period the average valuation of Korean banks was close to 1.2 times book value. Banks are usually valued as a multiple of net book value which means a multiple of the net shareholders' equity.

Our interaction with Standard Chartered executives was good, and we developed a high opinion of their team, so it was not difficult for us to transmit these feelings to the bank employees. It was the best possible option for KFB to be bought by an international bank that did not have an existing large Korean presence. Standard Chartered was the smaller of the two bidders but highly specialized in Asia and Africa since the eighteenth century. After this acquisition, Korea would become one of its largest national footprints, and that could be good for KFB employees, the classic case of being a big fish in a relatively small bowl instead of the opposite. Standard Chartered had a multinational management in which Koreans in the future could play a significant role.

The transition period was delicate, as always, as the acquirer prepared its new organization, convincing some executives to stay and fill the gaps. For me the main point was to arrive at an agreement between the union (and more generally the employees and officers) and Standard Chartered Bank, to avoid any disturbance, to keep the bank working, and to help start the new journey of KFB and its fifty-five hundred employees on the right foot.

I had to explain to the union what an international bank was, and to the SCB executives the realities of Korea: its labor organization, the employees' sensitivity, and their strengths and weaknesses in the new context.

SCB's early declaration that they were planning to grow the bank and increase market share while keeping the staff went a long way to reassure the employees and the union on this basic subject, but many other points had to be discussed.

I do believe that the trust the union chairman and I built played a major role in this long negotiation. Dozens of hours of meetings, many confrontations, and explanations were needed, .but it was worth it. The bank did not suffer any strikes, the employees were happy, and they began their Standard Chartered life with enthusiasm. The new management could focus on sales and organization instead of being totally immersed in labor fights like it so often happens in Korea.

In this process, one of the main issues raised was the name and the logo of the new bank. Standard Chartered needed to show its full support by integrating KFB into their family, and the employees wanted to keep the historical name, *Cheil Ouneng*. Finally, the logo and the English name (KFB had been used for decades, but only by foreigners) were going to be removed and replaced by Standard Chartered Bank's logo, but the First would stay and the historic Korean name would remain the same.

In sharp contrast with other mergers in Korea, the acquisition of KFB by Standard Chartered was executed without any strikes or demonstrations

Farewell Ceremony with Standard Chartered's CEO
Merwyn Davies and with KFB's Chairman of the Union
Hwan-Pil Kim

SCB First Bank

Chapter 7

Conclusions

After the turnaround story of Korea First Bank presented more or less chronologically in earlier chapters, as well as the multiple digressions to my personal observations and analysis on Korea, I feel it would be useful to make a synthesis of what I took away from this fabulous experience.

First, we will see the main lessons on the bank turnaround itself, then my views on the specificity of the Korean environment and its consequences, and then we will conclude with what struck me the most, my experiences of human relations in Korea.

Lessons on Korea First Bank's Turnaround

I do not believe in a quick paint job on a crumbling building. Cosmetic changes just do not work. A bank is a delicate organization, managing risks and making money on thin margins. Without a strong underlying structure, good results could not be sustained anywhere, but it is especially true in the cyclical Korean context. So we did not simply do a paint job. We totally rebuilt the bank from the foundation up like we thought it should have been, without shortcuts.

I was absolutely convinced of that, and so was the management team, but what made it possible was the full agreement of the shareholders. I remember vividly a discussion at the BOD on a large investment commitment and David Bonderman, the senior partner of TPG, saying, "If it is needed for the long-term good of the bank, we must do it."

After the decision to build, knowledge and techniques are critical in order to achieve that. Those are the specific strengths that a team of experienced professionals can bring from advanced countries where they have already seen the current stage of the evolution of the Korean banking industry elsewhere, in previous lives.

Techniques were needed.

IT and its processes had to be reliable and efficient, using the latest techniques of communication and real time. Without that, any industrial production is impossible and the production of mortgages (fifteen thousand loans a month) would have been impossible to sustain. More, the implementation of real time automated underwriting would have been a nightmare if our technology was not reliable. Stopping production and making the clients wait in a very competitive market would have destroyed our credibility and growth.

Processes should not only be efficient in a bank, but they need to allow for checks and balances, fostering strong controls and audit systems. The old Korea First Bank and its local competitor banks at their level of development during the crisis simply did not have any of these.

Flexibility also was critical. The IT system's architecture, the renewed core banking system, and above all the data warehouse, easily reachable and usable by different units' specialized software, played the most important roles in this needed flexibility.

It allowed a full range of suitable products and services to be designed, priced attractively, and marketed, quickly. Each one should be profitable but to follow up and act on we needed a sophisticated management reporting, tracking the losing products and the losing branches. This is what the data warehouse permit us to build.

Finally, a bank cannot work well without strong risk management. Counterparty risks, asset and liability and market risks have to be managed constantly. These are also techniques difficult to develop and maintain without deep experience.

But even when the techniques are definitely needed, they are not enough by far.

The actual strength of a bank (which is before all a service company) resides in its employees. The winners are the ones who are able to unleash this collective energy. In order to get there, a clear direction has to be decided and strong, even overwhelming, communication put in place to get all employees rowing in the same direction.

There is no successful marketing and by consequence no growth in banking where products are similar and competition fierce if the employee morale is low, if they are focusing on anything else than sale and marketing, if they are not rowing in the same direction.

The general understanding of and adhesion to the bank's goals was the most important step in rebuilding the fractured institution. To get there, the message had to be consistent in substance and in form and repeated endlessly.

In Korea First Bank's case, I defined clear growth objectives that allowed me to stop reducing staff and related costs. Continued focus on ERPs would have kept that as the major worry and would have kept our sales force de-motivated; I had to officially stop all layoffs and accept the temporary excess of staff as some additional marketing expense.

In countries where layoffs are easier, more usual (which means less dramatic and less expensive to implement), one way might have been to do it sequentially, a layoff period limited in time, followed by a growth strategy. That option was not feasible in the Korean context.

Similarly, the usual staff level in a bank is the one needed to service its clients and replace the ones leaving, but it would not be enough to grow aggressively. We tripled the volume of loans to clients in three years without reducing service. Banks that target a faster growth than the market need additional staff dedicated in attracting new clients, and the adequate staffing level for this growth strategy is quite different from cruise level.

Communication has to be loud enough and long enough to make its mark. I chose a simple three-year goal. I even added the total assets Won 40 Billion only because sheer size was important for the employees. Then I repeated it continuously and consistently until everybody in the bank absorbed it as if it were their own goal.

Communication and incentives are needed to unleash the collective energy, depending, of course, on the environment. In Korea, communication and emotional relations with the CEO and the bank were much more important than incentives. This would not be true in other countries.

The management team also plays a major role. Competency, cohesion, and consistency are the most important qualities to look for, but my experience running banks taught me how in vain the search for the perfect executive for every position could be.

The problem for the CEO is not to have the absolute best team. It is to have a very good team that worked together. A soccer team of eleven stars would be unmanageable and inefficient as the Brazilian team demonstrated some years, the best players bring poor results.

The main responsibility of the CEO is then to know the strengths and shortcomings of each executive and optimize the use of the team. The CEO should be able to give each one the responsibilities he can master and compensate for each one's weaknesses with his personal involvement or by changing the borders of each domain.

The Korean specificity

A tradition of womb-to-tomb employment and a very limited safety net outside of the company make staff reductions very difficult and traumatizing. That was the reason for the protective labor laws and strong unions inside large companies.

Koreans are less individualistic than Westerners and much more sensitive to collective feelings. That translates, in a positive environment, into a type of peer pressure that limits the number of vacation days taken, obliges people to work late and on weekends, and to give the maximum.

In a lay-off period solidarity develops with the victims, especially if there is a feeling of unfairness. This creates a low morale situation, general discouragement, an inferiority complex, and no marketing or sales. Globally, in good and bad situations, there is identification with the company or the employee-felt situation of the company.

In the Western world, cash incentives are the major way to orient and drive a sales force. Not in Korea. First, the environment has to be collectively positive, then the criteria and goals have to be very clearly spelled out and followed by management reporting.. Then, recognition becomes the most important incentive, with publicized awards for the best producers. Only afterwards, with less publicity, cash incentives may be added.

How to reach this collectively positive environment? It is based on the employees identifying with the employer/company and with the CEO, a very Confucian approach. The company is family, and the CEO the father. In this context, respect and adhesion mean high morale and cohesion.

The CEO must be an example for all to follow. He has to identify himself as the father figure and be an example by his time spent at the office, work habits (and many Koreans are workaholics), transparency, and above all, strong and consistent communication.

The reward is great. When confidence is built, employees feel reassured, and each success helps reinforce morale... Dedication returns, and everybody is proud to be part of the bank. From there, the results can be spectacular. Koreans love work well done and done on time, even without cash incentives. The CEO has to clearly define the direction, the ratios he considers important, and everybody then goes in the same direction.

Building personal relations without speaking the same language

Koreans have an original culture, strengthened and homogenized by over two thousand years of common history and isolation. Foreigners should not think they will react like them. They have to study Korean history and culture and try from there to get the ability to project what will be the Korean's reaction to an event or a situation.

Respect shown to a culture does not mean it needs to be mimicked, quite the opposite.

Koreans speak Korean. This language has more in common with the Mongol, the Japanese, and the Chinese than with any Western language. The difficulty to learn it is equivalent to the difficulty for Koreans to learn a Western language. Everybody is not born speaking English.

People should not be judged on their capacity to speak fluent English or even on their aptitude to understand English. Somebody expressing himself in a foreign language that he or she has not mastered often seems schematic or simplistic, but that does not mean they cannot be subtle in their thinking and when expressing themselves in their own language.

One of my worst memories was the hostility of some civil servants trying to demonstrate that foreigners cannot be any good. This kind of bad faith, objectively obvious, used to make me furious. But after some time, I had to admit that their attitude was caused by strong feelings of patriotism or nationalism, and then it was difficult for me to stay as angry, even if I knew them to be misguided and wrong.

When I arrived in the Far East, I was not aware of the high emotional level present in Korean relations. That was perhaps my most surprising discovery. These people, who were always trying to disguise their feelings while having such a strong sense of hierarchy, are in fact highly emotional. That was, when I think about it, the single point that for me made Koreans so sympathetic, and even today inspire me with fond memories.

The quality of relations we were able to develop without being able to speak directly in a common language was astonishing. As an example, I had the feeling after few months that S. H. Yang and I could understand each other even without an interpreter, without speaking any language in common, by our expressions and anticipated reactions. I had eventually the same feeling with H. P. Kim, chairman of the unions. But even with officers and employees with whom I never met one-on-one, the relationship and the emotions were obvious.

I will never forget the farewell reception a few weeks after the power transition. There was no more hierarchy, no more self-interest, but rather visible emotion showing the actual closeness felt by me as well as by the hundreds of employees and officers.

That was for me the most rewarding moment that I had not expected, nor even hoped for when arriving in Korea.